Collectors

Maya Gosens

Copyright © 2024 by Maya Gosens

All rights reserved.

No portion of this book may be reproduced in any form without written permission from the publisher or author, except as permitted by U.S. copyright law.

Contents

Chapter 1	1
Chapter 2	5
chapter 3	10
chapter 4	17
Chapter 5	22
Chapter 6	29
Chapter 7	35
chapter 8	40
chapter 9	46
chapter 10	52
chapter 11	60
chapter 12	68
chapter 13	74
chapter 14	83
chapter 15	88

chapter 16	94
chapter 17	100
chapter 18	106
chapter 19	119
chapter 20	124
chapter 21	129
Chapter 22	135
chapter 23	141
chapter 24	147
chapter 25	157
chapter 26	165
chapter 27	174
chapter 28	181
chapter 29	187
chapter 30	197
chapter 31	204
chapter 32	209
Chapter 33	223
chapter 34	228

Chapter 1

"Myra, come sit down." Said her Father. She smiled slightly and nodded, settling down next her him on the grey sofa. Her Mother joined her too, sitting down opposite them the other sofa.

"What is it?" She asked with slight concern lacing her voice. Both her parents looked at each other, silently communicating, before her Father sighed. "There is a proposal." He stated, gauging her reaction. Myra cleared her throat awkwardly, nodding for him to go on. "He's from a wealthy family. His name is Ben and he's 24 years old."

Myra nodded, glancing at her Mother. "Dad you know what rich people are like. They ask for more than we can offer. I don't care about his money-"

"That's the thing." He stressed. "He didn't ask for anything."

She immediately frowned at that. "Okay."

"Well there is one thing." Her Mother said softly.

"What is it? You know I hate the suspense you're creating." She said, shaking her head. "He has placed on condition as a part of the proposal."

"Mum." She bit out.

"Once you're married, you aren't allowed to communicate with us, ever again." Said her Father.

Myra's mouth dropped open, immediately standing up. "There's no way Mum. You're not expecting me to agree, are you?" She asked angrily. Myra was usually a calm person, she hardly let anger take control of her like this, but this was different.

"Sweetheart, you'll be happy." Spoke her Mother, giving her a grim smile.

"And what about you? How can I leave you guys and never speak to you?" She argued, feeling tears burning her eyes.

"You know it's normal for daughters to leave their homes-"

"Dad! We're not in the 1800s. I can't believe you even thought I'd give this proposal a second thought." She stated, clenching her fists tightly.

"Myra." Her Father said calmly, grabbing her hand and pulling her to sit down next to her.

She did so, but crossing her arms and not meeting any of their gaze. Her parents knew it wasn't hard for them to persuade her, they only wanted something secure for her. Her Father worked day and night shifts just to make ends meet and if this was a chance for his daughter to live somewhere safer and secure then they would never give it up. If they had a choice, they would keep her here forever, but they couldn't. Which was something that Myra knew too.

"We just want what is best you. We aren't going to be with you for the rest of your life. I need you to be safe as well as your sisters. I know you're working too, but I want to see you happy and I think it might be the chance for you." He explained gently.

"But Dad... how can you expect me to be happy without you? I'm happy here. How can I be happy not knowing how you're doing, how my sisters are? What if something happens and I never find out." She asked partially angry and sad.

"I'm sure he will let you know if that was ever the case, or let you reach out to us. Your Mother and I, think that this is a good proposal. Please think about it." He pleaded.

She pulled her hand out of his and left, walking into her small bedroom and shutting the door gently. She leant against the door, feeling a sense of heaviness come over her body, she felt hot and cold at once.

Myra stepped over to her bed and laid down, pulling her blanket around herself tightly, hiding herself, hoping that when she opens her eyes again everything would be normal, that this was a nightmare.

Tears rolled down the side of her face as she tried to keep her sobs quiet. She couldn't imagine her life without her family. Why did life have to be do difficult for her? No one else has to choose between their parents and having a spouse.

She felt like a burden on her parents, but they never thought of her that way. Myra was the most disciplined out of all of her siblings as well as the oldest, she hardly argued with them regarding any matter. Anything that needed to be done at home, she would to do it happily, whether it was financial or extra chores.

Her Father made sure to teach her basic life skills such as plumbing, cooking, when they had a car he made her change the brakes and engine oil.

He knew she was a bright child, but she didn't have a chance to prove it. She had studied as well as she could and her results her made her parents proud. She wanted to study further, do something with her life so they could get out of this poverty, but how could they afford it.

She couldn't apply for a loan, because they could see her Fathers finances, which were low. It saddened her parents, but Myra's smile didn't falter. She worked and helped financially, as well making sure she helped her mother at home with chores. She paid for her sisters finances too if she needed to, but no matter what she did, it is never enough.

Myra knew she had to give them an answer, she spent the next two days working like a robot, coming home and doing her chores and going to her room where she cried. She didn't bother eating Dinner, her parents were concerned. If they had another choice, they would never force her to choose.

Her Father loved all his daughters and he would do anything for them.

"Mum, Dad I have decided." She stated standing at the door of their living room. Both her parents head snapped up to look at her. This was the moment where she knew once she says yes, it would almost be impossible for her to get out of it. "Say yes, but I would like to speak to him and discuss my conditions and if he accepts then we will go through with it."

She was quickly embraced by both of them. "I'll let him know right away. I'm so proud of you." Said her Father with beaming smile on his face. She feigned a smile for him, before looking down again. "Don't forget my conditions." She said tightly. He nodded, pressing a kiss to her forehead.

Her sisters smiled at her sadly, hugging her tightly. "I'm going to sleep." She whispered, pulling away and leaving them to discuss the preparations they wanted to make.

She didn't want to be a part of it. She just wanted to spend the rest of the time with her family as happily as possible.

Chapter 2

Myra stayed in her room for the next few days again, avoiding all the wedding talk, but before anything was actually finalised, she had asked her Father to arrange a short meeting with Ben. Her Father asked her several times what she would ask, but she knew as soon as she told her Father he would tell her to stop.

She was dressed in simple jeans and t-shirt with her loosely curled hair tied in a bun. They decided to meet at a coffee shop nearby to her house. She waited in the shop, already settled down with her own drink.

"Myra?" Asked a deep voice. She immediately looked up to see a man fully dressed in a suit. He was a handsome man, but Myra could already sense that he only had looks working for him and no personality. "Hi. Please sit." She smiled gesturing towards the chair opposite her. Without another word he sat down. He didn't even smile back at her.

"What is it you wanted to talk about?" He asked, getting straight to the point.

"I have some conditions too, if we are able to agree to these then we can go through with this...'proposal'." She stated looking right at him. Myra was usually never so assertive, others may even say that she was shy, but she wasn't going to let this man think that he could dominate her.

He kept his face void of any emotion and nodded for her to continue. "My main condition is that I don't want any physical relationship with you until I feel I'm ready for something like that." She said carefully.

He stared at her for a moment. "Okay."

"Why don't you want me to see my parents after marriage?" She asked curiously, narrowing her eyes suspiciously. "I don't want any distractions. I am too busy and I need you with me at all times to attend formal parties." He answered.

"That's it? For such a minor reason you want me to avoid my parents? Am I missing something?" She asked confused with a hint of anger.

"I do not think you need me to tell you what your duties are as a wife. You can't spread yourself thin. If you cannot follow such a simple condition, then consider this proposal cancelled." He stated with an edge. Myra looked away, clenching her jaw and taking a deep breath.

"Besides, I am paying your parents 50,000 as a 'gift'." He added. Myra's eyes widened with shock. "They know this?" She asked.

"No. It will be a surprise transaction."

Myra bit her lip, it was a lot of money. If she married him at least they would spend some time in bliss, or somewhat less stressed. She couldn't help, but feel as if he was buying her and her silence. Could she sacrifice herself so selflessly for her family? She would do anything for them and she knew this.

"How can I trust that you will follow my conditions?" She asked.

"I can write up a short contract. If I break your conditions, you will have the right to divorce me. I expect you to go through with what I ask of you."

Myra stared at him for a moment, unsure of whether signing the contract would be more beneficial or dangerous for her, but if she states that he can't touch her then it meant he couldn't touch her under any conditions.

"Okay. I need some time to think."

"I don't have much time. You've got until the end of this week."

He stood up, gazing down at her with his striking blue eyes. "It was nice to meet you. Bye." And with that he turned around and left. She watched him leave the coffee shop, frowning at his strange behaviour. "How stuck up can someone even be?" She muttered to herself. Surely he isn't that important.

She finished her drink and walked home, wrapping her arms around herself. All she was continuously asking herself, whether it was worth it. Would she be selfish if she said no? She'd never spent more than the usual school hours away from her parents, how can she suddenly abandon them, even if they tell her to.

Why couldn't she meet someone that wanted her without any conditions? Was it so hard? Her parents found each other before they turned twenty and had her. They didn't care about wealth, why is it so important now?

She avoided any conversation with her parents about their meeting. Myra knew that no matter how much she wanted to refuse, she couldn't. Maybe they could work things out after they get married, perhaps build their relationship.

It would take time, but if she was going to marry this man, she would have to get to know him better. Her mother always told her that you had to be patient to deal with men and with time their minds and their hearts soften.

It made her question her ideology though, surely if a man loves you he would be willing to compromise just as a woman would. Sometimes she didn't believe what her mother said, especially now that she was going to get tied into a relationship. Things were different back when her parents met, nowadays relationships were just based on sex, or looks and maybe reputation.

Days blured past as she stayed in the room. Her parents knew that she was conflicted, but they weren't forcing her. All they wanted for her was happiness and security.

She knew she didn't have much time left now. Part of her just wanted to say no, she knew her heart didn't agree to this, but it was a step she had to take for her family. It would be one less person that her Father would have to care for. One less expenditure. One less person to feed.

She opened her bedroom door and walked to her parents room keeping her head down. She raised her hand and knocked, waiting for them to allow her to come in. When she heard her Father call her in she opened the door. "What's wrong Myra?" Asked her Father with a frown.

"You can say yes to him." She said quietly. She knew that the wedding day would come quickly, her days in her house were numbered.

Her Father jumped out of bed, pulling her into a tight embrace. "You have made me the happiest Father ever." He said proudly. Myra felt tears well up in her eyes. "How can I live without you Dad?" She asked.

"Myra, my sweet child. I love you. We all love you and we all want you to be happy. Just remember that." He said, his own eyes filling with tears.

"What if I'm not happy there?" She asked, wiping her eyes. "My daughter, you are always welcome back here. I will never force you to live with a man who hurts you, but can you promise me that you will try to understand him, try to live with him?" He asked, looking down at her.

"I promise, dad." She sobbed, nodding her head. Myra couldn't stop her tears from flowing, all she could think about is the fact that she had to leave her home.

After a few minutes of staying in a tight embrace, Myra excused herself, not wanting to cry in front of him anymore. She walked back to her room, laying down in her bed and pulling her blanket over her head. Her Father had already given the news to Ben and were most likely discussing the wedding plans.

She closed her eyes drifting into an exhausted slumber, hoping that it was all a nightmare and she would wake up and everything would be normal.

----

chapter 3

The wedding plans were made in a haste, he wanted it to happen within two weeks. Her parents didn't have to worry about much though, he had brought her wedding dress tailored to her size, booked a venue, but limited to a few guests.

Her sisters rushed around her, trying to do her hair. Myra did her own make up, firstly because she couldn't afford to find a makeup artist, secondly because she didn't want a cake face.

Her wedding dress was simple, but classy. It hugged her figure perfectly. The sweetheart lining showcases the illusion lace across the sleeves and neckline. The skirt was made of satin, tight around her waist forming into ball gown.

They held an outdoor wedding. It was beautifully presented, no doubt Ben had taste and class, hence why he chose a beautiful bride for himself.

Myra lightly dusted herself with a long lasting powder and applied a nude pink lip gloss to match the natural shade of her lip.

"I think this is it..." she sighed, refraining herself from biting her lip incase she ruins her gloss. A habit that would surface every time she was nervous or anxious, at times giving her a noticeable bruise.

Both her sisters nodded, gulping down their emotions. They knew if they cried now then their sister would not be able to stop herself either. She was mature, but extremely sensitive and everyone knew that. She couldn't bare to see anyone cry, it would bring tears to her own eyes, whether she knew them or not did not matter.

Her relationship with her siblings was normal, they would argue and then next minute they laugh until their insides ached. She gave them a tight smile and all of them could feel the emotional tension in the room.

"Myra, are you ready?" Asked her Mother peeking her head through the door. "Yes." She answered, looking at the floor. "I just need to put my veil on."

Her Mother nodded, smiling at her. Myra lowered herself as her Mother draped the veil over her head. These traditions weren't theirs, but Ben wouldn't have been happy to follow theirs and they knew that.

"I'll send your Father over, okay?" Myra nodded plainly. Her Mother rushed out wiping a tear that had escaped. After a few minutes there was another knock on the door and she knew it was time.

"You look gorgeous. All of you." He said, smiling proudly, he had to hide the pain of not being able to see his daughter. Myra didn't say anything, she couldn't get any words out of mouth.

The ceremony was going to be extremely short, to her it seemed that this was just a formality. They were going to say their vows and that would be it. She spent the last few days with her siblings and parents as much as she could.

The sound of the orchestra playing softly interrupted their moment together. Her Father held out his arm for her, she took a deep breath linking her arm with his. She kept her eyes down as they made their way down the stone path which which was lightly covered with petals. Her heart was racing in her chest, there was no way she could back out of this marriage now. It was too late.

The wedding was picture perfect. On either side of the aisle there were chairs placed, enough for 30 guests. Surprisingly, Ben only invited a few friends, not any family. Myra would've loved the small intimate event if she actually felt anything for him, but she was still willing to give him a chance and get to know him.

True love can change hearts. That's what her parents always said. Her own Father was a rebellious man when he was younger, but as soon he met his wife, he changed his behaviour to become better for her. Her gentleness, her kindness and purity of heart attracted him most. These were the same characteristics that Myra had inherited.

Myra and her Father walked down the aisle with Sara and Nayma walking behind either of them holding flowers in there hands. The sun shone brightly and the weather was warm with a gentle cool breeze occasionally. The closer she walked to him, the weaker her knees felt.

She had finally reached him. Her Father released her arm and Ben turned to look at him and shook his hand.

Silence fell around them as the notary stood beside them now.

"Dearly beloved, we are gathered here today to join this man and this woman in holy matrimony.

Ben Smith, do you take this woman to be your wife, to live together in matrimony, to love her, to honor her, to comfort her, and to keep her in sickness and in health, forsaking all others, for as long as you both shall live?"

"I do." He answered plainly, his voice not holding any emotion.

The man then turned to Myra "Myra Rahim, do you take this man to be your husband, to live together in matrimony, to love him, to honor him, to comfort him, and to keep him in sickness and in health, forsaking all others, for as long as you both shall live?"

For a moment Myra lost her voice. She squeezed her eyes shut tightly and took a deep breath.

"I do." She answered weakly.

"Repeat after me." He said turning towards Ben again.

"I, Ben Smith, take you Myra Rahim, to be my wife, to have and to hold from this day forward, for better, for worse, for richer, for poorer, in sickness and in health, to love and to cherish, till death do us part."

Ben repeated the lines as if reading out a statement, just mere words. As their ceremony passed, she felt thay perhaps Ben was not a man that could ever accept her fully as an equal partner.

The notary again turned towards her and repeated her vows to her.

"I, Myra Rahim, take you Ben Smith, to be my husband, to have and to hold from this day forward, for better, for worse, for richer, for poorer, in sickness and in health, to love and to cherish, till death do us part." She repeated just audibly. Her voice shook as she linked her fingers together to keep then from shaking too much.

'Love.'

Would he ever love her as he promised in front of these people?

"Please place the ring on the bride's finger and repeat after me. 'I give you this ring as a token and pledge of our constant faith and abiding love.'"

With those words he slipped a diamond ring on her finger.

"Please place the ring on the husband's finger and repeat after me. I give you this ring as a token and pledge of our faith and abiding love.'"

Myra repeated the vows once again, this time much clearer as she began getting a hold of her emotions. It was inevitable.

"Please join hands."

Myra held her shaky hands out in front of him and he grasped them rather gently.

"By virtue of the authority vested in me under the laws, I now pronounce you husband and wife."

She froze at the next few words that left the Nortary's mouth.

"You may kiss the bride."

Ben released her hands and they dropped at her sides, limply. He lifted her veil and Myra looked up at him. He stared at her as if silently questioning her. She sighed, giving him a subtle nod. He leaned down and Myra shut her eyes tightly as she felt his lips press against her own.

Her face heated up with embarrassment of being kissed so publicly. She was sure even her Father wasn't looking. They had always been very private about intimacy, but they could see the love for each other in there eyes.

A round of applause startled her, as Ben pulled away and grasped her hand turning towards the crowd. Myra's stomach churned, it was time for her to leave.

"We are leaving in 10 minutes." He stated low in enough for her to hear as he continued to smile at the crowd.

She glanced up at him almost frowning, but kept her face blank. They both walked down the aisle, he let go of her hand and walked over to his friends and Myra looked up at her parent's, who were already in tears.

Now she was unable to stop herself. Her eyes flooded immediately as a continuous stream of tears flowed down her cheeks. Her family rushed towards her and pulled her into a tight hug. Myra sobbed harshly, unable to believe that this will be the last time she will see them until Ben doesn't change his mind. And from what she could sense already, it was highly unlikely.

Her Father pulled her against his chest, she cried even harder as she felt her Father shake with emotion. "Myra, my sweet daughter. You are strong, remember that. No matter what happens, you will get through it. I love you."

"I don't want to leave Dad." She sobbed wrapping her arms around him tightly. "Myra, don't think this is the last time you're seeing us. You will see us again, one day."

Obviously he would try to be optimistic, but Myra knew he was only trying to ease her sadness. She hugged her Mother who was crying just as uncontrollably as her.

"Be brave Myra. I love you as well." She whispered, giving her a watery smile, this only made her emotions worse. Smiling whilst tears run down your face is the hardest thing to do. She knew she would have to learn it if she wanted to face her future.

After her Mother, came her younger sisters who couldn't believe that they wouldn't see her. She was their rock, whenever they needed extra money they would run to Myra for help who would generously help them. She would even work overtime to get them what they needed. Myra wrapped her arms around their shoulders, pulling them close to her.

"Take care of yourselves. Study hard. Don't forget about your parents." Were the last words of wisdom that she was able to say through her tears.

"It's time for you to go. Ben's waiting." She wiped her face with the back of her hands, not caring that she smudged her make up. Ben walked over to her Father, again shook his hand and hugged him and exchanged words of reassurances.

When they were done, Myra held on to her Father's hand as Ben grasped hers. She wished that her Father stopped her. "Let's go."

Ben pulled her away from her Family. Her hand slowly slipped out of her Father's as he gave her one last reassuring squeeze and smile. They all hugged her Father as they watched Myra leave. She felt as if everything was happening in slow-motion, yet at the same time so fast.

A sleek black car pulled up beside them. Ben opened the door for her and Myra sat inside keeping her teary eyes on her Family. Ben came around the other side and shut the door. Myra stuck her hand out the window, hoping that somehow they would be able to stop her from leaving.

But the car started driving away.

Myra slumped back in her seat as they disappeared out of her vision, crying all over again. Ben held out some napkins for his weeping wife, giving her no support yet not telling her to stop.

She closed her eyes, turning away from him.

Only hoping that this was just a nightmare she would wake up from.

chapter 4

She began adjusting to her life with him. It had been two weeks since their marriage and her life has been unbelievably quiet. Ben goes to 'work', comes back home, eats dinner and goes to sleep. He doesn't even talk to her unless it is to complain about something. It was strange, she had asked him about his job and he would just say he works at an office, not clarifying what he does specifically. She wondered if her Father knew. She was saddened at the thought that perhaps her Father didn't know what he did for a living and assumed it was something good.

Myra tried her best to keep herself busy in his house. She couldn't call this her home, she felt like she didn't believe here. Often she thought about her family and how they used to do their chores together, even her Father. Her extended family mocked her Father for helping out by saying it was a woman's job, but he didn't care. He loves his family more than anything else in the world.

Myra learnt to control her breakdowns, it terrible during the first week. Tears would well up in her eyes while she ate, but she would quickly wipe them away. She hated the silence. There was always some kind of commotion in her house, whether it was laughter or fights. Sometimes she thought that she heard someone call her, it almost sounded like her

Mother. She felt as if she was going crazy. Here, he would only greet her and unless she asked him a question he wouldn't talk to her. He gave her a whole list of rules he expected her to follow, she felt more like maid rather than a wife.

But she obeyed.

She promised her Father that she would try to work things out between them, but if her Father found out about how he treated her, he would've told her to comeback to him. Unfortunately, it was too late. She wasn't even allowed to speak to them, nor see them. And they would never find out.

There would be no way they would ever 'bump' into each other, they lived too far from her home. Yet it made her think, how could she try to like a man that hardly looked at her and even when he did, it was to complain about something she wore, or that a strand of hair was out of place.

He made her throw away all her clothes and replaced them with dresses that were tailored to her size. She was glad she didn't bring all her clothes, most of her favourites were still at home. She'd never worn a dress before, especially so publicly, and most of the dresses were really short. She had worn maxi dresses, but they we're modest. She felt too exposed around him.

He expected her to wear them from the morning until it was bedtime, in case someone would come to see him, she has to look presentable enough so she wouldn't cause him any embarrassment. That wasn't all though, she had to wear heels too, but when she complained about it, he said she has to learn to do everything in heels. rush around make food, laundry. She was surprised he didn't tell her to shower with them on, at least at that thought she almost laughed.

Just like that she fell into a monotonous and dull routine. She sat at the Dinner table waiting for Ben to come home again. She tried to follow the etiquette of a proper housewife, be happy when he comes home so he forgets his problems, but part of her felt that maybe she was his problem, or maybe part of it.

After a while she heard Ben's footsteps making their way towards the Kitchen. 'Finally.' She thought, she didn't like eating alone, which meant that she completely misses Lunch everyday. Although, she wasn't completely happy, she tried her best to be the wife that he wanted her to be. "Hey." She smiled.

"Hi." He answered, not bothering to look at her. Her smile faltered, but she stood up to serve him his food. Myra made Shepherd's pie with a piece of boiled chicken and fresh leaf salad as a side. He began eating and Myra filled her own plate up with a piece of chicken and salad. She poked at her food for a few moments until Ben spoke up.

"I think I've given you enough time to adjust. I've been invited to a formal party this week and I need you to accompany me. Please don't wear those cheap dresses, wear something modern, preferably short and black." He said looking up at her finally. Myra brushed her feelings off at what he said and nodded obediently.

"Who else will be there? What kind of people?" She asked hesitantly, hoping that he wouldn't embarrass her again.

"Some friends and business people. You are free to drink and mix with people. Just don't do anything embarrassing." He said, continuing to eat.

"Okay." She answered quietly. She didn't drink anyways, so he wouldn't have to worry about embarrassing him.

She had a few bites of her food, her appetite had disappeared after what he said. He didn't have to be so harsh about everything for no reason. Ben didn't seem to notice that she stopped eating, or perhaps he didn't seem to care enough to ask her about it.

He did tell her to lose more weight, but Myra was already thinner than she was on her wedding day. It wasn't her fault that she was slightly more curvy than the women he had seen around himself. Her stomach had a gentle curve to it, to any other man it was extremely attractive, but to him it was just fat. Her body was perfectly hourglass, gifted at the top and bottom. She knew there'd be no way she could get rid of those curves.

He finished his food and left the kitchen silently, going up to their room. Myra sighed sadly, biting her lip hard. How could she get him to like her when he didn't even like looking at her.

She picked up her plate and threw her food in the bin, if she were at home she would've definitely been told off for wasting it, but what was she going to do with food that she didn't even like to eat.

Doing chores was nothing new to her, in fact she enjoyed it when she was at home. Her sisters would have a laugh in the kitchen whilst cleaning, keeping each other entertained until they had finished everything. She rinsed the plate under hot water before squeezing soap over the sponge and cleaning it. Even though they were just surviving at home, they were happier than ever, happier than most families that had money.

Once she had finished washing up all the dishes that she had used, she went up to their room and changed her clothes before laying down on the far end of the bed. They even had separate blankets. It made her wonder, if she had allowed him to create a physical relationship with him, would things still be this way?

Part of her knew it would've been this way regardless. He didn't find her attractive. It would have just another duty added to her list, which she would have to fulfil as an obedient wife. She hugged the blanket to her chest and closed her eyes before her eyes would well up with tears again.

So... I'm kind of back.

Here's another sad chapter of Myra's life. It's making me sad too, kinda feel like my married life is gonna be dead like that too. LOL

Anyways, let me know what you think. Ben is a piece of shite. I'm still trying to figure out how he fucked up, then you guys will know too.

Please remember to Vote, Comment and Share my story if you like it. It means everything to me.

Z.A.B

Chapter 5

To say she was nervous was an understatement. She wasn't sure what to wear to the party that wouldn't make her feel too exposed, but also not too modest just because Ben didn't like that. She looked through the variety of dresses that he had got tailor-made for her, none which she would ever willingly wear out alone. At least he gave her an option of wearing what she wanted at home, she couldn't imagine having to wear fancy dresses at home, for no reason whatsoever.

She finally decided after long minutes of staring at her cupboard, pulling out a black dress. She already didn't like it, just because of the sleeves. She quickly pulled the dress on. It was an off the shoulder dress, tightly fitted. Due to her extra curves at the top and bottom, it was tight in those areas, making some cleavage pop up from the dress and accentuate her hips more than usual. She already felt an embarrassed blush covering her face although she was alone, it would be much worse if she were around strangers that she would meet at the party.

She sat down at her vanity, deciding to put her hair up in a bun, but letting a few loose bangs decorate the side of her face. Finally, it was time to do her make up, she kept it very light. It was easy to overdo a look like this and ruin it. She applied a thin layer of nude pink gloss and finished off the look with some eyeliner. She got up again and took out black strappy heels. She gave herself a once over in the mirror.

She liked the way she looked.

But she would've preferred being dressed like this if she was going to be alone with her husband, being so bare felt very intimate to her, but Ben had no interest in her. She grabbed her purse and walked down the stairs to meet Ben.

He was sitting on the sofa, sipping on some sort of alcohol drink. "I'm ready... I think." She stated shyly. Ben stood up, giving her a once over. "You look perfect." He stated, her blush increased even more. It was the first time he had said anything nice to her.

"We will have to be somewhat affectionate in public, Myra." He stated as he stood in front of her. She nodded understandingly. He raised his hand in front of her and gazing down at her with his striking blue eyes. She lifted her hand and placed it in his, feeling even more shy than before. He held her hand in a firm grasp and led her out to his car, opening the passenger door for her.

"People will ask you questions so be prepared to answer them with confidence. If you are confident then there will be no problem, but the moment you stutter, they will catch on to that and intimidate you. So at least for your reputation, please be confident and pretend to know what they are talking about even if you don't."

Myra looked away again with embarrassment, she didn't have a degree specialising in anything, but she educated herself enough to learn about different topics. He didn't mean to offend her this time at all, she could tell that much.

"Okay. I'll try my best." She nodded, looking out of the window and watched as they drove through a narrow road. The rest of the ride was quiet, and they soon arrived outside a mansion. It was huge, bigger than Ben's. The pathway was decorated with tall iron lampposts, lighting up the way to the entrance of the house. It looked completely magical, behind the lampposts there were thick rose bushes.

"Wow." She muttered, as her wide eyes took in her surroundings. "Just wait till you see the inside." He smirked. He grasped her hand again, this time linking their fingers together as the double doors opened and they stepped.

Myra's mouth dropped open as she looked up at the chandelier, lighting up the hall dimly, surrounded by smaller chandeliers covering the ceiling. She looked out in front of herself to see small groups of people mingling together, holding glasses of champagne or wine. "Do I have to drink?" she asked, glancing up at him.

"No, I'll order you something non-alcoholic, don't worry." He said as he began pulling her though the hall. There weren't many people, if she had to guess, she would say around 50-60 people scattered around the hall.

"We're going to meet the owners."

Myra quickly shut her mouth and cleared her throat. They walked towards a small group of people at the end of the hall near the grand stairs. Everything looked like it was out of a movie. He stopped and tapped the man on the shoulder.

He turned around and greeted him with a big smile. "Ben, I see you have finally made it." He said, shaking his hand. "Meet my wife, Brenda." He said introducing his wife. The man was older than Myra expected him to be, regardless she gave him a soft smile. He leant down to her level and gave her a holy kiss on either of her cheeks. "Oh." She mumbled shyly, unable to help herself. He pulled away with a smile. Next was Brenda and she did the same and Myra attempted to greet her the same way, earning her another small smile. "It's lovely to meet you, Myra." She said warmly. "It's nice to meet you too, Ma'am." She said, looking at the woman. She was older too but kept herself maintained even at that age. She had dark brown hair, pulled into a loose braid and wore a form fitting dress, with a silver stone belt around her narrow waist.

"So polite! Please call me Brenda." She laughed, waving her hand in the air. Myra smiled and nodded. They began talking about work and Myra zoned out, but with a squeeze of Ben's hand she was pulled back into reality and looked up at him.

"I'll be around then Jared, I'm sure you're busy hosting the party." Said Ben nodding, shaking his hand again. "It was nice to meet you both." Added Myra with another shy smile. Both of them nodded fondly.

They began walking away, towards another small group of people. "They seemed to really like you." He said tugging her gently. "Who are they?" she asked looking around the hall. "My Boss." He stated. Myra's eyes widened. "Why didn't you tell me?" She asked, surprise lacing her voice, but making sure her voice remained loud enough only for him to hear.

"They can spot pretentious behaviour from a mile away."

'Would they be able to spot their fake relationship?' She thought as they continued walking. He wrapped an arm around her waist, pulling her closer as they neared another group of people, but this time younger. Most of them seemed to be single as other men had women in their arms, similar to how Ben was now holding her.

"Look who made it!" Said one man, stepping forward and giving him a side hug. Thankfully, he was the only one that came forwards to hug him and the rest just shook his head.

"Meet my wife; Myra." He introduced and all their eyes snapped to her. She blushed again. "Hi." She said looking up at them.

"Where'd you get her from?" asked one of the guys with a smirk. Myra immediately felt embarrassed, she felt like an object in front of them. "We met through common friends, and quickly got married." He said, giving her a soft smile. Had he been genuine, she was sure her heart would have raced at the way he was looking at her, but she knew all this meant nothing. Even the slight hope she had earlier at his house had vanished.

She smiled in response, keeping herself in check as he leant down to kiss her on the cheek. "It's nice to meet you, beautiful." Said another one as he grabbed her hand and kissed it gently. "Oh, thank you." She said smiling awkwardly.

He was obviously flirting with her; she could tell by the look in his eyes. The way he looked down at her, his eyes lingering over her exposed skin, then for the first time that night she dirty. She wasn't used to being dressed this way, she felt exposed. She wanted to shy away, but Ben told her they would pick on her weakness.

"It's nice to meet you too." She answered coolly. She looked at the other women around her, some seemed to really be smiling and others were sour. They were jealous, they knew she was the most beautiful woman to step into the hall tonight, her curves caught the attention of many men around her, but she remained oblivious to them.

The men soon separated from the women and Ben left her there with a group of strangers. "What's your name?" asked the brunette, she seemed nice, she was one of those few women that smiled at her.

"Myra. What's yours?" She asked, attempting to strike a conversation.

"What kind of name is that." Said another brunette.

"Probably a name with more meaning than yours Brittney." Said the nice one, rolling her eyes, but winked at Myra. She bit back a smile.

"Let's go somewhere else before these bitches cremate themselves with jealousy." Smirked the brunette, grasping her hand and pulling her away from the women. "By the way, my name is Meerah." She added after they were a few feet away from the other group who were still glaring at her.

Myra nodded politely as they stopped near the bar area of the hall. "What do you want?" She asked smiling at her. "Anything non-alcoholic please."

"Of course, let's get Pomegranate Mojito Mocktails." She suggested. They quickly ordered their drinks and clanked their drinks together making her giggle. They were quickly pulled into a conversation, discussing their marriages. Unlike Myra, Meerah was happy with her marriage and her husband loved her very much despite the bumpy start they had, with him constantly trying to get into her pants.

Myra didn't want to overshare her sad married life, she wasn't sure if she could completely trust her, but she did hint that their marriage was dry. Meerah only nodded sympathetically but said that it takes time for couples to understand each other. Her husband quickly interrupted their conversation, glaring down at Myra.

She gulped, looking away. She didn't have anyone to hold her securely. "Oh, stop it Zaheer. This is Myra, Ben's wife." She said introducing her to her husband. He was a huge guy, very tall, broad and dominating.

Recognition glinted in his eyes and he gave a her a half smile, which she returned awkwardly. Despite how nice Meerah was, Myra didn't like this sort of gathering. She felt like a display piece, everyone stared at her like she was an alien and perhaps she was. She was too simple for them, too polite and most of all, her wealth didn't meet up to their standard regardless of what Ben had.

Thankfully time passed quickly between the three of them talking together. Zaheer was pretty nice once he opened up a little bit.

"There you are Myra." Muttered Ben as he wrapped his arm around her waist. She jumped startled, looking up at him. "We have to get going now." Myra nodded gladly, smiling at Meerah apologetically.

"It was nice to meet to Myra. You should come over sometime." She said pulling her in for a hug and she nodded. "Of course."

They both said their goodbyes and exited the mansion, walking to their car. Their drive home was silent and Myra couldn't wait to get out of these clothes and slip into her t-shirts and sweatpants.

She dove into bed, once again thinking about her sad life and having a husband that doesn't even love her. She wondered if he was even attracted to her. Surely if he was then he would try to something .

She closed her eyes and fell asleep, exhausted from a long boring business party.

I'm back guys! Late as usual. (Oops)

I live in a house full of people and none of them except my younger sister knows that I write as a hobby, so when they ask me what I'm doing I usually have to say 'nothing' lol.

But here is the update. I hope its not boring. This chapter is essential though. Shows you how shitty Ben is.

Let me know what you think!

As usual please Vote, Comment and Share.

Z.A.B

Chapter 6

Myra let out a huff of frustration. How could he have expected her to organise a whole event on her own. Not completely, but she didn't know what to do. Most she had ever done was probably for twenty people, he is inviting 60. He only took her to that event so that she could see what they do and then host one for his house too, it had already been two months since that party, how was she meant to remember anything.

She had to make sure everything was ready by 6pm and it was already 3 o'clock. She went downstairs and overlooked all the people in the house, starting with the kitchen. There was nothing more important than the snacks and drinks. Thankfully Ben hired some chefs to make those, but she was sure next time he would expect her to make those. She didn't like these pretentious gatherings, these weren't done for any good causes but to show off their wealth.

"How long until the starters are ready?" She asked the chef, crossing her arms. Like Ben said, she had to fake confidence; in other words, pretend to care about this event. This event was going to drag on until midnight, she could already feel it.

"All the food should be ready by 5.30, including cleaning up and setting out the buffets." He stated looking at her. "Okay, that's great. Thank you." She smiled before going into their main hall where they were going to hold the party. The tables were set up and people were rushing around, trying to set up and the lighting. "This is such a waste of money." She muttered to herself, before she walked up to the Supervisor with the clipboard.

"Hey, I hope everything will be finished on time." She stated, keeping her expression stoic as she looked at the middle aged woman. "Yes, it should be done on time. So far everything is happening according to the schedule. Should there be any problems, I will let you know. We should be finished by 5 o'clock." She said, her eyes skimming over the clipboard as she spoke. Myra nodded, trying to remember if there was anything else left to check on.

There were going to be servers around the hall, but it was Ben's job to contact them so she didn't think much of it.

She wandered around until 4.30 and watched as everything was eventually put together and it looked beautiful. Regardless of the beauty of it all, it was missing a motive for her. She walked back up to their bedroom and slid her cupboard open searching for another dress.

Her eyes caught an Emerald coloured satin dress, the only problem with it was that it was full-length and she was afraid that Ben won't like it. He didn't giver her any preference this time. Myra rolled her eyes at her own thoughts, 'Shouldn't have brought it, if he didn't want me to wear it.'

She quickly changed into the dress, looking at herself in the mirror. It was an off-the-shoulder dress with a slit going down the side of her leg. She grimaced, no wonder he brought it. Nevertheless, she liked the dress, it looked very elegant, it made her feel a little more secure that the one she had to wear last time. She slid open her other cupboard and tried to match a pair of heels to go with it. She decided to go with silver pumps, they were holographic, which she loved. Myra disliked jewellery, but decided to wear some simple dangly earrings to match with her heels. She finally sat at her dresser and did her makeup, just like last time.

Just as she stood up Ben walked in and looked over at her, letting his eyes trail over her dress, it curved around her nicely. Myra felt embarrassed, not shy. She didn't even feel butterflies, nothing that she read in romance books. He was only looking at her because he wanted to find a flaw in her. "You should leave your hair out, but fix it so it's not all over the place." He stated walking into the bathroom. She bit her lip and sat down again, letting her hair fall in waves. She combed through it lightly, trying to make sure she doesn't puff it up. The only time she brushed her hair was when it was wet, otherwise the curls would mess up.

It soon was 6pm and both of them slowly made their way down, where some guests had already started arriving. Myra stood close to Ben and eventually he linked their fingers together as they were now getting approached by his guests. Myra just smiled and would answer if she was asked anything. Soon she was surrounded by similar faces, yet unfamiliar. They were the same people from the last party. She masked her face, planting a fake smile on her face as she shook hands with the men. One man squeezed her hand and her eyes snapped up to him, it was the same man from last time. She gulped nervously, Ben was oblivious to what the man seemed to be doing. She felt disgusted and tried to pull her hand out of his as subtly as possible.

He eventually let go, giving her a dirty smirk and winked at her. Myra narrowed her eyes at him, before looking away and glancing at Ben who was busy in another deep conversation. "Myra!" She heard a high-pitched excited voice call out to her. She turned her head to where she heard the voice from. She smiled brightly, finally someone she knew. "Meerah."

She walked over to her and was pulled in a tight hug. "Are you alright?" She asked softly. Myra nodded, feeling embarrassed that she noticed it. "It's okay. He's an asshole. Still hasn't learnt his lesson after getting beaten up by Zaheer." She muttered while pulling away.

"Oh? Is that what he is usually like?" She asked naively. Meerah nodded plainly, giving the guy a glare. "Everything looks great! When I had to hold my first gathering I messed up on so many things." She laughed.

"Was your husband not angry?" She questioned, slightly concerned. She snorted unattractively at her question making Myra giggle. "He knew I have no interest and I told him before, that I'd be shit at it. So now he organises them himself." She stated. "Which was part of my plan, but it turned out worse than I thought."

"I knew it!" Grumbled a deep voice from out side. She looked to the side and her eyes widened as she noticed Zaheer glaring down at her. Myra watched apprehensively, afraid that Meerah would get into trouble. She smiled up at him, looking somewhat embarrassed at being caught. He walked over to her, wrapping his arm around her and pulling her back against his chest before leaning down and whispering something in her ear. Myra looked away feeling like an intruder, but heard her gasp which caused her to look back at her to see her husband leaving with smirk on his face and Meerah staring at his retreating figure with her mouth open.

"Is everything okay?" She asked softly, pulling Meerah out of her daze. She snapped her mouth shut and looked down even more embarrassed. "Is he angry?" She asked again. Meerah looked up, fanning her face with her hand before she sighed.

"Everything is fine. He's just... annoying." She said with a smile. "Don't worry about it Myra. He knows I'll kick his balls if he even thinks about hurting me, which he wouldn't do. He's like that." She reassured, holding her hand and squeezing it reassuringly. Myra nodded gave her a smile. Even though part of her was concerned she could sense that they had good chemistry, even now while they were talking she noticed her taking subtle glances at her husband.

They continued talking lightly until Ben had come over to them with Zaheer. Ben was saying something to her, but she watched as Meerah lent up to her husbands ear and whispered something before pulling away. Zaheer's eyes widened for a moment before he gave her a dark look.

"We're leaving now." He stated, not taking his eyes off his wife who just smiled, before looking Myra. "It was great seeing you again. I hope I see you soon." She said, pulling Myra into another hug. "Is he going to hurt you?" she asked fearfully. She pulled back with a frown, shaking her head at Myra. "I'm going to have my wedding night tonight." She whispered in her ear, pulling away with a grin as Myra gasped. She watched as Zaheer dragged her away from the party. Meerah turned to give her a wave before matching her husbands pace and running off.

She finally turned her eyes to Ben who seemed to be annoyed at her. "Sorry." She mumbled looking down. She wished she would have a relationship like that. She'd never seen her parents openly flirt with each other, but she knew they loved each other a lot.

"The party will be over soon. You need to clean up." He demanded. Myra's mouth dropped open, unable to stop herself from frowning as she looked up at him. "I'm not doing it today. How would you expect me to wake up the next day on time to do other things." She answered. Why couldn't he be like other husbands, or at least pretend to care about her.

"I don't care. It's your job." He stated before walking away. Myra felt her chest feeling heavy, she couldn't cry yet. She took a few deep breaths, before joining him again and bidding their guests goodbye.

Pretty soon his house emptied and as the last guest left, he immediately walked up the stairs, not waiting for Myra. She walked up and slipped out of her heels, placing everything where it was before, grabbing her clothes and going to the spare bathroom and changing into her t-shirt and and shorts that reached her knees.

When she came back to her room she saw the bathroom door open but he wasn't inside. She frowned, but before she could react the bedroom door slammed open and a man stood there with a gun in his hand.

Heyyyyy!!!! Finally I had time and motivation to write the next part and you all know what will happen next!!! Just saying though, there will be some changes in the next chapter in terms of dialogue just to make it flow better. So yeah... I'm gonna upload this now. lol

Also Zaheer and Meerah was an idea that I had ages ago and thought to introduce them here, haven't really written much for them though.

Please don't forget to Vote, Comment and Share.

Z.A.B

Chapter 7

"Did you really think that you could get away with lying to me about your little party. Maybe if you knew how to communicate like a fucking man, this wouldn't have happened. Give me my money." Growled Vincent. He was dressed in an expensive suit, his hair was gelled back, keeping a slight puff at the top of his head. "Vincent, I don't have anything. Please give me time." Ben pleaded on his knees as his guards held him down.

Another of Vincent's men stepped forward cocking his gun and pressing it to his forehead. "Take my wife!" He screamed out of terror. She was his prized possession, absolutely stunning and innocent. She was just his trophy, a beautiful show case for his friends. She listened to everything he said. It had only been two months since they got married and she had no clue what her husband was up to.

Vincent grabbed his guards wrist, pushing it down. "Find her." He demanded lowly. He had seen her once, only briefly at the last gathering. He waited patiently staring at Ben coldly, he felt sorry for her, from what he had seen she was kind and gentle with everyone.

He heard whimpers of pain as he saw his guard dragging her down from upstairs, jerking her forwards so she fell down beside her husband. She looked at her husband, feeling confused and embarrassed. She panted with fear and looked up at Vincent, noticing the gun attached to his hip.

"Take her and spare me. Do whatever you want with her. She's a good fuck." Begged her husband, pushing her forwards roughly, falling forwards again, bracing herself quickly before her head hit the cold tiled floor. She landed beside his expensive polished shoes, gasping, feeling hot tears rolling down her cheeks. She was shocked that her husband threw her to another man, he knew she had never been touched before.

Vincent crouched down to her level, grasping her chin between his thumb and forefinger, pulling her face up so she looked up at him. He smirked down at her cruelly "Go and pack your stuff. No funny business, I'm sending my guard with you. You do anything wrong, he will kill you."

She sobbed, slowly standing up and walking back up to their bedroom, feeling the guard following her closely. She took a deep breath when he stayed outside of her room. She wiped her tears pointlessly, as another fresh wave rolled down her face. She pulled out her suitcase, filling it up with all her clothes and some of her personal belongings, such as her Mother's jewellery and a family photos.

She looked down at the ring she wore on her finger, taking it off and throwing it on the bed. She zipped her bag up, looking down at her clothes, she was already in her pyjamas, but now she wanted to change. She was wearing shorts and a t-shirt.

"Can I please change my clothes?" She asked softly.

"If you do. I'll drag you out naked." He stated smirking at her. She bit her lip, holding back her tears, wrapping her arms around herself.

The man walked in grabbing her suitcase and rolling it on the cold floor. "Let's go." He demanded roughly, she quickly pulled on her slippers and walked out after him.

"I'm taking your wife. If you want her back, give me my money. You have six months, if I don't get it back, then the least you can do is prepare for two funerals, but if I get bored of her expect me back sooner." He threatened, staring down at Ben with a sick smile.

He looked back up to see the young woman shaking with fear after hearing his threat, her eyes were wide with terror. "Let's go." He grunted, turning around and leaving. All she could do was follow him silently, he signalled her to sit in the car and walked to the other side settling down. She squeezed herself against the door, keeping as much space between them as possible.

His car was warm, but she still shook, not because she was cold, but because she was so scared of what he would do to her. He stared at her shivering body, unable to stop his eyes from trailing down at bare legs and then over her over the rest of her body. She was beautiful, Ben was stupid to let her go.

They didn't speak throughout the ride. They walked into his mansion, she stopped at the door looking around, if she wasn't held hostage she would have been in awe of his house. A young maid, almost the same height as her, walked up to her. "Let me show you your room." She said smiling at her.

She nodded, crossing her arms and following her up the stairs and down the dimly lit corridor. She opened the door and stepped in, gently urging her in the room. "You'll be staying here." She smiled, before walking out and shutting the door behind herself.

She sat down on the edge of the bed, but quickly stood up when she saw the door handle get pushed down. Vincent walked in, shutting and locking the door before locking eyes with the beauty in his room. As he walked further in, he noticed her panting with fear and staring up at him with wide eyes.

"What's your name?" He asked firmly, staring at the young woman intently. "Myra." She answered softly, trying to stay calm. "Are you really as good as your husband claims, Myra?" He asked, stepping closer to her. Myra's knees shook with fear and shook her head desperately. "H-he lied. He's never touched me." She whimpered softly, feeling her heart pounding in her chest.

"Has anyone touched you?" He asked curiously. She shook her head again before answering weakly "No."

He hummed, keeping his eyes stormy eyes on her face, watching her lips tremble with nervousness and fear. "Lie down." He demanded coldly. She quickly laid down on the bed, hoping whatever he does with her would be gentle.

He was surprised at how quickly she obeyed him. He pulled his coat and shirt off, and then his pants, hanging them up behind his door. He moved over her, parting her legs and leaning over her, she fisted her hands into the bedsheets, closing her eyes tightly. "Does your eagerness mean you want me to fuck you?" She gasped softly, hearing his crude language and voice so close to her.

"I just don't want you to hurt me. I'll be good, just please..." she sobbed, biting her lip hard to keep her cries as quiet as possible. "Please what?" He asked, sliding his hand under her shirt, feeling her shudder under his touch.

"Just be gentle. Please. Please." She begged looking up at him as tears continued to overflow from her eyes. He slid his hand out of her shirt.

He tightened his jaw and moved away from her, laying down near her, keeping some distance between themselves. He sat up and pulled the blanket over her and over himself. Myra sobbed softly, relieved as he moved away from her. She was still afraid, what if he is playing games with her, what if hurts her while she sleeps? "Sleep Myra." He demanded, laying on his back, placing his arm behind his head and looking up at the ceiling for a moment before closing his eyes.

She hoped he would have some mercy on her as she turned away from him and closed her eyes. She was unsure of how long it took her to fall asleep, but eventually forced her body to relax and fall asleep beside him.

Here is the next part, not too different from the original. I hope you guys enjoy reading it again.

Also, I was thinking about writing the next chapter in Myra's P.O.V. Let me know if you want to keep it third person or Myras pov.

Please remember to Vote, Comment and Share!!!

Z.A.B

chapter 8

Myra P.O.V

My eyes fluttered open as daylight poured in from the huge window. I stretched myself, before sitting up and rubbing my eyes. I threw the covers off myself and stood up walking into the bathroom. I yawned, thinking of what kind of breakfast to make for Ben, otherwise he'd complain about eating the same thing again. I reached out for my toothbrush and frowned when it wasn't there. I looked up taking in my surroundings.

My eyes widened as last nights scene played out in my mind.

I was taken by a man.

I heard the door behind me open and quickly turned around to be faced by the man who I shared the bed with. As much as I tried to control myself, I felt myself begin to panic as his words echoed in my head. 'If I get bored of her, expect me back sooner.'

He kept his piercing grey eyes locked with mine. I was unable to look away, frozen with fear.

"Spare toothbrush is under the sink. The towels are in the cabinet and your suitcase is under the bed." He listed before falling into silence. I watched as his eyes trailed down my body making me squirm uncomfortably.

I took a sharp breath as he took a step forwards. He didn't stop. I stumbled back against the sink looking down and closing my eyes tightly, hoping when I open them he wouldn't be there; hoping that this was all just a nightmare.

I could feel his body heat radiating off him and jerked back when I felt his fingers grasping my chin pulling my face up to his. I opened my eyes and gulped at his proximity. My whole body shook with fear. I clenched my hands into fists to control the shaking, but I couldn't.

"I expect you down as soon as you're done. I have some things I want to discuss with you." He said in a low threatening voice. I nodded, biting my lip hard to keep myself from making any sounds.

He let go of my chin and I quickly looked away, closing my eyes tightly. I heard his quiet footsteps moving further away and the door shut softly.

A violent sob left my mouth as my knees gave out from underneath me. I pulled my knees to my chest and cried. I couldn't believe Ben just gave me away without a second thought. I hoped that maybe I could make some space in his heart. I did nothing, but agree to every word of his and asked for nothing in return.

Now any chance of me ever seeing my parents is over. The thought made me cry even more. I couldn't find it within me to get up and freshen up, but the threat in his voice was echoing in my ears.

I pushed myself off the floor and grabbed a towel from the cabinet. I quickly stripped and made sure that I washed myself fast in case he decided to walk back in.

Even during my shower I felt tears pouring down my face. I walked over to the sink, brushing my teeth with the spare brush, putting it in the empty holder.

When I walked out, I noticed that my suitcase was already pulled out from under the bed. I quickly opened it and pulled out a decent dress and my undergarments, quickly walking back to the bathroom.

Once I had finished changing my clothes I brushed my wet hair before using my towel to dry it without tangling it up again. It took me 45 minutes to make myself look presentable.

I walked down the stairs walking into the lounge area but it was empty. I then walked towards the open door on the side, leading me to a spacious kitchen.

I froze once I saw him sitting at the counter, holding his gun and wiping it with a white cloth. "Come sit." He said without looking up at me.

The stool was too close for my liking, but I had no choice at this point. My heart was pounding and I began feeling light headed out of fear. I sat down on the stool facing him, placing my hands in my lap. He pulled my stool closer, pushing his legs between mine, parting them causing my dress to slide up high enough to make me panic.

"Don't move." He demanded in a rough voice. I froze feeling my breath coming out faster than usual.

He gripped my wrists in one hand, his skin felt rough on me as he tugged me forwards holding them down between my spread legs. In his other hand he gripped the gun, sliding the cold muzzle over my thigh. I panted, looking up at him with wide eyes, gulping audibly. He smirked down at me cruelly, clearly enjoying tormenting me.

"How long have you known your husband?" He asked as he trailed the gun higher at a slow pace. I tried to answer, but no words were coming out of my mouth. He narrowed his eyes at me, pressing the muzzle against my throat firmly. I whimpered, closing my eyes tightly.

"I'm waiting." He growled angrily. I felt tears filling my eyes as I tried to answer him again.

"T-two m-months." I answered shakily.

"How long have you been married?" He asked again.

"Two m-months."

I panted with fear, my mind wasn't able to focus on anything he was saying.

"P-please move the gun. I-I'll tell you everything." I begged, hoping he would listen, but I knew it was highly unlikely. I've probably put myself in more trouble.

He moved the gun and I opened my eyes, feeling tears running down my face. He kept his face stoic.

"How did you meet?"

I sniffled, looking down as I answered him.

"My father introduced him to me."

"Your father was probably involved too then. Where does he live?" He asked. I panicked shaking my head at him. "He- He doesn't know anything. Someone told him that Ben was looking for a suitable match. We got married within a week." I quickly explained.

"And I'm supposed to believe this bullshit of you marrying someone you don't know?" He sneered angrily. It was was as if his eyes had darkened even more. "Yes." I whispered. "I had a choice, yet I didn't at the same time."

He didn't say anything which was surprising, I thought he would taunt me. "Do you know anything about him?" He asked, sounding not as angry as before.

I shook my head. "He never told me anything." I said quietly, feeling embarrassed. "You know why?" He asked mockingly.

"Because he has nothing to tell. He's a fraud. All that money he shows off, is mine. He's just a fucking secretary at a basic office. Even that house, he brought with my money."

"I'm sorry." I apologised, even though I hadn't done anything wrong but be associated with him.

"What's your pathetic apology going to do?" He asked tugging me forwards angrily. I gasped as more tears rolled down cheeks and flinched away from him. I tried to pull my hands out of his grip, but he widened his legs more, causing mine to spread too. I panted and fought him, trying to keep legs closed.

"Please! I'm sorry. Please." I begged again, as I stopped fighting him. The more I fought him, the more force he applied.

I finally looked up at him only to see him glaring down at me. He clenched his jaw tightly and released me slowly. I let my hands drop down limply, as I sobbed quietly.

He reached over the counter grabbing something. I froze, was he getting his gun?

I flinched again as he pulled something in front of me again. I looked down to see a box of tissues in his hands. I hesitantly reached for it as I looked up at him. When I was satisfied he won't move I pulled a couple out and wiped my face quickly.

He stood up from the stool, walking away from me towards the door. "You better pray that your husband can return my money in six months. I don't think I need to tell you what will happen afterwards. Empty your suitcase, there's space in my cupboard. Lunch will be ready in a hour and I expect you to be here on time." He stated, turning around to glance at me. I nodded, and watched him leave.

As soon as he was out of my sight, I broke down even more. He was a monster. My wrists were bruised and throbbing with the tight grip he held me with. My legs ached from being kept forced open. I looked down shamefully, my dress rode up high enough for him to see what I was wearing underneath.

I stood up carefully onto my shaky legs and walked back up to his room to do what he had told me to. He wasn't there thankfully and hoped I wouldn't see much of him.

Sooooo, let me know what you think of their first day together.

Vincent was just extra mean to poor Myra.

Writing in first person is so hard once you get used to third, so if you see any mistakes just point them out. Thanks.

I'm excited to write this book and I hope you guys like what I have planned. Things are going to get heated pretty quickly now.

Anyways, please Vote, Comment and Share.

Also thanks to everyone that followed me!!!!

Z.A.B

chapter 9

Myra was beginning to settle in. It was easier for her to accept her fate rather than fight it. She wasn't going to fight what was going to happen to her anymore, but hoped that there was a higher power who would help her out.

She walked down to the kitchen, it was nearly lunch time again. Just as she was about to sit at the counter she noticed another man with his back to her. She froze.

He turned around after hearing her walk in. Myra gasped with fear. It was the same man that threatened her. He smirked, taking a step towards her.

"Stop." She pleaded weakly, she couldn't stop her natural reaction to him. It would take time for her to learn to not react to them.

He paused, not expecting such a reaction. "Woah. Calm down." He said lifting his hands up. She didn't listen and instead backed away from feeling tears filling her eyes. She bumped into something hard and turned around to see Vincent right behind her.

Vincent wrapped an arm around her waist to keep her from moving any further. "Please don't hurt me." She whispered as she tried to move out from his grip, but he pulled her tighter against himself.

"What the fuck did you say, Sam?" He asked, sounding more annoyed than angry. "Nothing man. She freaked out." He said rolling his eyes.

"Myra, what did he say?" He asked looking down at her. She gulped fearfully.

"H-he threatened me..." she hiccuped.

"Oh come on. It was on the day you kidnapped her." He stated crossing his arms.

"What did you say to her?" He asked narrowing his eyes. "I said if she changed her clothes then I would take her out naked in front of everyone."

Vincent tried his best not to glare at him and took a deep breath.

He released Myra, but she continued to back away. "I'm sorry Myra, it was all part of pretending to be a scary man. I wouldn't have hurt you." Said Sam.

She looked up at Sam hesitantly to see him grinning down at her. "Please? I'm sorry. I'm not really that horrible I promise."

She looked up at Vincent who was also staring at her with his piercing eyes. He gave her a subtle nod, clenching his jaw. She looked down defeatedly.

He took a step towards her and grasped her wrist gently, making her gasp.

"I'm Sam by the way. I'm the cool one, obviously Vincent is the hot headed one. If you don't believe me, just look at his face." Said Sam without looking back at him. Myra looked back at him once again to see him glaring at Sam. Myra would've laughed if the circumstances were different, but quickly looked away when his glare towards her. Her heart skipped a few beats, almost choking on air.

He tapped the stool next to himself, urging her to climb on next to him. She sat on the stool silently, looking down at her lap. "It's your turn to serve food Vinnie."

"Stop fucking calling me that." He growled, before placing the food on the counter. Sam just chuckled before grabbing a plate for Myra and serving her chicken and vegetables on the side with gravy. Myra didn't talk, she was afraid. Even her Dinners with Vincent were quiet unless he wanted her to do anything or ask something.

She lifted her knife and fork cutting into the piece of chicken and dipping it into the gravy before taking a bite. She chewed the bland food swallowing each bite without focusing on the taste. Her mind reeled back to her family dinners, where they all worked together to prepare a meal, sit together and laugh. Her Father would always have some sort of story to tell then of his childhood.

She could feel her chest beginning to feel tight with emotion. She tried to control her emotions as much as possible, holding back her tears, but it seemed that she wouldn't be able to do it anymore. She wanted to hide. She felt tears slowly sliding down her cheeks. She tried to discreetly wipe her tears, but peeked up at Vincent who seemed to have noticed her crying, but he didn't say anything. She felt pathetic.

Sam noticed that she stopped eating and looked down at her, frowning. "Come on Myra, the food can't be that bad?" He joked lightly, but it only set her off even more. She released a sob.

Sam rubbed her back comfortingly, also feeling sympathetic for her situation. Vincent watched her wipe her tears again, there was something so child-like and innocent with the way she wiped her tears, it was adorable.

A word that he never used to describe a woman. She didn't care that her mascara was running down her face, or that her face was becoming red.

Sam wasn't sure if he should touch her anymore in case she gets scared again, but he didn't want her to cry. He stopped eating and wrapped his arm around her, turning her stool and pulling her face to his chest. Myra didn't fight him, instead she clutched him tighter to himself. She was surprised that she found comfort in his embrace.

"There, there. It's okay Myra. Just let it all out." He soothed. Myra heard Vincent move from the other side of the counter and tensed. He was probably angry at her for ruining their lunch, she waited for him to do anything, but nothing happened.

She pulled away after a few minutes hicupping softly. "You don't need to be scared Myra. We're not as cruel as you think." She wasn't sure if she believed him, but nodded anyways. "Finish your food." He said letting her go.

"I-I'm not hungry." She whispered softly. "That's fine. Go upstairs and relax for a bit." He smiled, but she kept her eyes on her lap and nodded before climbing down carefully and making her way out of the kitchen. She paused for a moment. Vincent was probably up in his room.

Would he get angry at her? She had been crying for the past few days, even if she had accepted her life here. Her heels clicked on the hard floor as she walked up the stairs, pausing outside his room. She slowly pulled the handle down and opened it, before stepping inside and shutting it again.

Vincent stood by his cupboard, with his shirt unbuttoned. She looked at him as she turned around. Her eyes widened briefly when she noticed his bare chest. "Sorry." She squeaked, turning around to face the door, feeling a hot blush rising on her face.

She'd never even seen her husband shirtless. Vincent cornered her against the door. "Myra." He said. She jumped hearing him so close to her. She took a deep breath before turning around to look at him. He was now slowly buttoning up his shirt.

"Yes Sir?" She answered softly. He didn't like that she didn't look at him. He gripped her chin, tilting her head up so she looked up at him. She was still trying to avert her gaze, but he held her firmly. "I'd prefer if you look at me when I'm talking to you and when you answer me."

He saw a brief flash of fear in her eyes. "Sorry." She apologised again. He released her chin, but this time she kept her eyes on him. "We're going shopping today." He stated.

"Shopping?" She asked confused. "Yes. I'm sure you need some sanitary things?" He asked and watched her blush again. "Oh..." she muttered.

"We're leaving now. Do you need to get ready?" He asked moving away.

"Just five minutes please." She answered softly. He nodded, knowing that it wouldn't take her such a short time. Myra walked into his bathroom, quickly washing her face with cold water before drying it with her towel.

She stepped back out and looked at him meekly. "I'm ready." He nodded for her to follow, knowing that this was going to be a long day.

13.05.21

Since I couldn't upload the other book, I decided to do this one.

I hope you guys like it. The next chapter is going to be a little bit cute and Vincent is going to get a little naughty. □

Please don't forget to Vote, Comment and Share.

Z.A.B

Also Eid Mubarak to my Muslim readers.

chapter 10

The ride to the shopping centre took an hour. Myra was dressed in another black ruched dress and black heels. She had no idea where he was taking her.

He placed his hand on her lower back gently, walking her towards the lift in the underground parking. She looked at the small poster in the lift and her eyes widened. He took her to one of the most expensive shopping centres in the UK.

The lift dinged and they both stepped out. He stared at her as she took her surroundings in with wide eyes. "Why are you looking around like you've never seen anything like it?" He asked, scoffing at her. Myra looked down again embarrassed. She had never been to a place like this, her mother usually did her shopping. She loved going out though, but after her marriage she only went out once for that party.

Vincent watched the blush rising on her face and narrowed his eyes, not saying anything else. He grasped her hand gently pulling her to the ladies section. She looked down at their joined hands and blushed even more. He picked out a floral short dress for her, holding it up against her. Myra looked at the price tag. "No!" She gasped.

He looked up at her with confusion. "What?"

"That's too expensive." She said pushing it away.

Vincent gazed at her for a moment. "These are on me."

Myra still continued to shake her head, refusing to even touch that dress. Who was stupid enough to pay £1.5k for a dress?

"Myra." He said in a low voice. "Can't we go somewhere normal?" She asked softly, looking up at him. God, he was so tall.

"Normal?" He questioned, squinting at her.

"Yes, like Primark, or something else." She said looking down.

"What's that?" He asked and Myra looked at him shocked.

"It's a retail shop, just 90% cheaper."

"Later. First finish here." He said moving down the aisle. What's the point of later? She argued in her mind.

He continued to grab dresses and move along. Myra decided to look around at other things, not realising that she walked away from him. She looked at the jewellery. She loved minimalistic jewellery and they had exactly that. She looked at the ring, it was a square aquamarine stone, with a silver band.

She stared at it for a moment. "Wow." The more she looked, the more it sparkled. A sharp tug on her wrist pulled her out of her thoughts and she gasped loudly. She looked up at him he squeezed her arm painfully hard. She whimpered in pain, feeling tears stinging her eyes.

"Already trying to escape?" He growled, it seemed his eyes were darkening with each word. "No." She whimpered pained. He didn't let go of her arm, but loosened the grip on her as he walked towards the clothes section again.

She looked around, but luckily no one had seen the exchange between them. She bit her lip harshly, trying to keep up with his long strides.

He walked around a little more, continuing to pick up dresses from the racks before stopping outside the changing rooms.

"Try them on and show me. Every single one of them." He ordered, throwing the clothes on the bench. He pushed her inside the changing room, settling on the bench right opposite her room. He leaned back, pulling his phone out while he waited.

Myra picked up the first dress, it was a simple white dress tight around her waist and flaring out at the bottom. She took her heels off and pulled her dress off, pulling the white one on. She zipped herself up and looked at herself in the mirror. It was beautiful, so smooth and soft, sort of understanding why it was so expensive.

She pulled the curtain away and stared at the floor. When she looked up at him, he gave a small nod of approval and Myra closed the curtain again.

She couldn't remember how many times she changed or how many dresses there were, but felt tired. There were so many different colours, she liked the tones, some were pale and some were warm. She put on the second last dress, looking a the last dress. No way, was she going to wear that.

The dress she wore now was blood red and bright, it was obvious that she didn't like it. Although, it hugged her perfectly, she wondered how he managed to pick the perfect size for each dress. She moved the curtain away, looking at him. He squinted at her, looking her up and down. He shook his head disapprovingly. "This is the last one." She lied shakily.

He smirked, catching her out immediately. "I have given you seventeen dresses, you have only worn sixteen."

Myra's mouth dropped open, unsure of what to say. She pouted closing the curtain and pulling the red dress of and holding the floral one, the first dress he picked up. He waited impatiently now, tapping his shoe on the ground.

She pulled the dress on carefully, clasping it shut carefully from behind. It was shaped with a sweetheart neckline, that left nothing to imagination that's how low cut it was. The sleeves were beautiful and voluminous. It was too revealing, apart from the bra like clasp around her back nothing else covered her, up until where the skirt started around her lower back. In other words, she was practically naked.

"I'm waiting." He grumbled, from the other side. Myra's hands shook as she slowly moved the curtain to the side. She was unable to look at him as she stood before him, wrapping her arms around herself.

She had taken much longer to move the curtain away for this dress, he knew she was trying to put it off. His eyes took in every inch of her curves, the dress hid nothing. Her breasts were squeezed against the soft cloth, plumping them up more than they already were. She peeked up at him through her lashes and their eyes met. He lifted his finger, twirling it, signalling her to turn for him.

She wanted to refuse so badly. She took a deep breath feeling her heart pumping wildly. She gave him a slow twirl, glad that he hair was covering her back at least.

"It's t-too revealing, S-Sir." She stuttered. Vincent stood up abruptly, frightening her. He took slow steps towards her, Myra panted nervously, stepping backwards. She backed away until there was no where to go. Her body was going into overdrive with mixed emotions when she saw him close the curtain behind himself.

What was he doing? Would he ...? Myra gulped as her throat suddenly felt parched. He turned around, gradually closing the gap between them. She closed her eyes tightly as she felt his proximity.

Vincent carefully took hold of her hand, linking his fingers with hers pressing it into the full-size mirror behind her. Her other hand fisted the skirt of the dress. She was short, only reaching up to his chest without her heels. He leaned down, grazing his stubbled cheek against her reddened ones, hearing her breath hitch. He went even further down, nuzzling into her neck inhaling deeply as he placed his other hand on her bare waist.

She felt hot, so hot. Her skin felt as if it was on fire. It made her bite her lip hard, definitely hard enough to bruise them. His hand slid up higher, caressing her over the dress, stopping below her breast. He pulled away from her neck, looking down at her. Her soft skin was glowing in this lighting, her cheeks remained rosy the whole time. He could feel the heat her body was emitting, surprised that she hadn't pushed him away.

Her chest rose and fell faster than usual, feeling his mouth water at the sight of them. He turned her around pressing her front into the mirror, keeping his hand linked with hers, but twisting it behind her back. Myra pressed her forehead against the mirror, shivering as she felt his fingers on her shoulder, moving her lustrous hair off her back.

This time Vincent bit his lip at the sight of her toned back. She gasped she felt his warm hand down her bare back, unintentionally arching into him as he pressed his thumb into her adorable back dimple.

He had to stop, he had to, before he did something that he would regret. He let of her hand, pressing both his thumbs into her back dimples.

"We're definitely getting this one." He murmured against her ear. She gulped audibly.

"I- I won't wear it." She argued weakly. He turned her around. "What did you say?" He asked, in a tone which made her change her answer. "Nothing." She whispered.

"Change." He demanded walking out. Once he stepped out he took a deep breath, adjusting himself quickly. She stepped out a few moments later not waiting for him and walking on. He could carry those dress himself if he wasn't going to listen to her.

Vincent walked in and hung the dresses over his arm before following her and then walking in front of her, leading her to the till. The lady at the till stared at Vincent while she checked out the items for him.

"Your total is £15,498." She stated. Myra's mouth dropped open and was ready to protest. He shot her a dark look and she quickly looked down again, complying. How was she supposed to pay him back for all that? He held her bags and they walked back to the elevator.

She refused to to say anything to him, let alone look at him. Her mind drifted back to a few moments ago and shivered as she felt heat blossom in her stomach again. How could she have let him come so close to her? She could've screamed, shouted, but even though she feared him, she didn't tell him to stop. He touched her so gently, as if she would break. It felt as if could still feel his hands over her bare skin.

Vincent watched her closely and noticed that she was deep in her thoughts, biting her lip and shudder slightly. A warm blush covered her cheeks again.

He wanted to know what she was thinking.

She shook her head at herself and sighed.

They walked back to his car and gave the bags to his driver before settling down. Myra opened the passenger door and sat down, facing away from him keeping her arms crossed.

"Where do you get your sanitary things from?" He asked. She kept her mouth shut, knowing her defiance would get her into trouble.

"Myra." He threatened. She took a sharp breath turning to look at him. "Any local drugstore." She answered.

"Name." He demanded.

"Boots, Superdrugs, Savers." She listed. He faced back to front letting the driver know where they were going to go next.

When they came at their next stop she stepped out, suddenly feeling too overdressed for the shop. He followed her in as she walked straight to what she needed, grabbing a packet.

"Take more. I'm not going to have time to come every week." He stated annoyed. She didn't want to be one of those hoarders, but he was right, she should be grateful that he allowed her to leave the house, unlike Ben.

She picked up four packets in her arms and walked up to the till. Vincent grabbed a basket and grabbed her arm. "Myra. Buy everything you need." He said holding the basket out in front of her. She placed the things in the basket and walked over to the different things she needed. She didn't take longer than fifteen minutes which surprised him, he'd been shopping with his previous girlfriends and they took their time.

After that Vincent took her to 'normal' shop where she picked out some tshirts and sweatpants to sleep in. Vincent looked around, keeping an eye on Myra as she picked out her clothes. He saw a dress that he liked that he wanted her to wear. It was short and not something she usually wears. They regrouped when Myra walked up to him, indicating that she had finished.

They were done faster than he expected and it was almost Dinner time. "Are you hungry?" He asked as they walked back to the car. Myra just shook her head. He sighed and they settled down in their car making their way home. The drive home was silent, neither of them knew what to say. He leaned his head back closing his eyes.

A/N 20.05.21

So I decided to update this a day earlier and hopefully you guys like this chapter.

It was the cutest shopping trip ever.

I actually hate shopping with a passion. If I want something I'll order it online or go in store and literally buy that one thing. What I do like, is going to big stores and playing hide and seek. I already feel sorry for my future husband.

Anyways, please Vote, Comment and Share.

Z.A.B

chapter 11

Myra was still upset and had her occasional breakdown. Obviously, she tried not to cry in front of him, afraid that her constant crying would annoy him, but he would say nothing and instead would leave a box of soft tissues next to her.

After their spontaneous shopping trip he spent time out most of the time, but before that he gave her a tour of his house, letting her know where the laundry room was and any other places that she might need to use. He even had a swimming pool in the back.

She sighed, all she did was sit around all day and go join them for dinner. She'd never had so much free time, even in her parents house; there's always something to do.

"Myra." He said causing her to jump.

"Yes Sir?" She asked gently. She wasn't really sure if she was allowed to call him by his first name, but she wasn't going to risk anything.

"I am going to have company over today. I need to you to serve drinks to them. Dress appropriately." He ordered, giving her a once over. She didn't know what appropriately meant. She mustered up some courage and looked up at him. "What would you recommend I wear?"

He looked down at her, before walking to her cupboards where she kept her clothes. He stood there for a good minute before pulling out a black dress and holding it up. She blushed looking at the skin-tight dress he was holding out for her. She immediately regretted asking him, but nodded taking the dress out of his hands.

His lip twitched, almost smiling with amusement. She dressed modestly, even to bed, where most women prefer wearing tank tops and shorts.

He was shockingly not bad to live with, she'd assumed that he would do what he brought her here for.

"Be down by 8." He ordered, walking out of his room and shutting the door behind himself.

Myra looked at herself in the mirror once, smoothing out her black dress and brushing her fingers through her soft curls. Her dress was short and both sleeves were off the shoulder, reaching a few inches below her bottom. The neckline gave a good view of her cleavage.

She walked down to the kitchen and took a deep breath, pulling out a tray and neatly lining up ten beer bottles and a bottle opener.

She stepped out into the lounge, keeping her head down as walked towards the men. They were all roaring with laughter, cussing each other.

She held the tray out in front of the men, and they all took their bottles one by one and they mumbled their thanks to her. As she got closer to Vincent, she tightened her grip on the tray, praying she does not drop anything. She glanced up at him as she bent down over slightly holding the tray out in front of him. She looked up at him as he nodded at her, trying his best to not blatantly stare at her exposed cleavage, but as she stood up he let his eyes wander over her curvy body.

"Would you like me to get you anything else, Sir?" She asked softly. "Get more beers and leave them on the table." He ordered. She nodded biting her lip, clutching the tray to her chest. As soon as her back was turned, he almost groaned at the sight. Her dress hardly covered her shapely legs and her heels only made them look more toned and longer. Her bare shoulders enticed him, her golden skin made his mouth water, he just wanted to mark her, leave love bites wherever possible.

She brought another round of beer and bent down to place it on the table. "Ah!" She yelped at the burn of harsh slap on her ass, straightening up immediately. She instinctively placed her hand on her backside, rubbing it as her face burned with humiliation when the whole room of men laughed at her.

She looked at Vincent again, feeling tears burn her eyes. He kept his face blank. Her lip trembled as she turned around and ran out of the lounge followed by the sound of howling laughter.

She ran up to the room closing it and sobbing. She had never felt so violated.

As soon as she left the room he stood up and everyone fell quiet. He marched over to the man that had dared to touch her, grabbing his collar roughly. "This is your first and last warning. If you even fucking look at her, I will shoot your eyes out. This goes to all of you." He threatened, glaring at any man that dared to look up at him.

"S-Sorry Boss." He stuttered pathetically.

He let them stay for another hour or so, discussing their next target. When they all left, he slowly made his way up his room opening it. As soon as Myra heard the door handle move, she scrambled off the bed and ran to the joined bathroom locking the door. He heard her running into the bathroom and waited for her to come out, although he was not sure what to say.

He had not meant for anything like that to happen to her. Obviously, his men were not aware that she was not like their usual server, who happily allowed men to touch them.

"Open the door Myra." He demanded, knocking on the door. She trembled on the other side of the door; knowing she was in trouble.

She stayed on the other side of the bathroom unable to get her legs to move. "Open it, or I will break it." He threatened. She gasped with fear, slowly walking over, unlocking the door and opening it. He grabbed her forearm, pulling her out and pushing her up against the wall.

"Turn around, pull your dress up and place your hands on the wall."

She shook her head desperately, looking up at him pleadingly. He held on to her arm turning her around rather gently. "Are you going to do the rest or shall I?" He asked, running his hand over her spine. She grabbed the hem of her dress slowly rolling it up, baring her plump backside. He cursed under his breath. He looked at the red handprint on her left cheek, feeling his blood boil. He should have punched him instead.

He moved away, grabbing a small tin from his bedside drawer, dipping his fingers into it. He rubbed it over red handprint, feeling her tense up. It took everything in him to not squeeze it in his hand and spank it himself. Her ass was perfect for a good spanking. She gasped as the cooling effect started to take place.

"What is that?" She asked quietly.

"Cooling cream."

"W-Why do you have it?" She asked again. He smirked, turning her around.

"I like to spank women." He stated and watched as her eyes widened with fear. "You hurt them?" She whispered looking at his face. "No. Spanking can be pleasurable, if done right and if your partner enjoys a little pain."

She did not believe a word he said. 'Women like getting hit?' She gulped audibly. Would he hit her?

As if sensing her worry he sighed. "Pain and pleasure is consensual. Partners discuss this beforehand. This punishment is for women that purposefully tease their partner, that are naughty, that enjoy being bad. Nothing for a prude like you."

She looked away embarrassed. "I'm not a prude."

He chuckled lowly, placing his hand on her bare thigh, dragging it higher until his fingers touched the lace of her panties. He hooked his fingers into the side, watching her intently, her breathing quickened as she looked up at him.

He looked down between their bodies as he pushed his hand higher up, cupping her breast over her dress.

"Stop!" She gasped. He smirked, keeping his hand in place. "I thought you're not a prude." He taunted, placing his other hand beside her head. "Why?"

"You're not my husband." She whispered, turning her head to the side.

"And if I was?"

She swallowed nervously. "But you're not."

"So why hasn't your husband?" He asked.

"I... -" She wasn't attracted to him. He was not unattractive, but she could not force herself to like him much. They had a cold relationship.

"Has he never touched you?" He asked moving his hand away. He rolled her dress back down, keeping her pressed against the wall, stepping closer. "Not even here." He stated, brushing his thumb over her lips, as they parted under his touch.

She shook her head quickly "Only on our wedding day." He hummed in response tilting her head back, so she looked up at him.

"One day I'm going to make you scream with pleasure."

Myra's eyes widened as she gasped. "Mmm, you're already gasping." He teased. She quickly shut her mouth and looked to the side as she blushed.

He was pleased by her reaction, at least she was not running with terror. He smirked, pulling away from her and grabbing his pyjamas and walking into the bathroom.

She heard the shower running and pulled out her own clothes, changing into the them before he came back.

She tied her hair loosely before she went to sleep, otherwise it would be sprawled out all over the bed.

She liked her hair long, but now she was debating on cutting it off, the last time she cut it short when she had constant headaches which was 3 years ago, since then she just gets it trimmed slightly every year. It reached her waist now and maintaining it was expensive. Maybe she could get the maid to do it for her.

She sighed, climbing into his bed staying close to the edge. A few minutes later he emerged from the bathroom, drying his hair quickly. He laid down close to the centre of the bed, looking up at the ceiling again.

There was a moment of silence between them.

"You should've punched him." He said suddenly. Myra turned to look at him with surprise. "Isn't he one of your men?"

"Doesn't matter." He muttered. "I didn't... I thought... I would get into trouble." She mumbled.

"So if I forced myself on you, you would allow it?" He asked turning to her. Her eyes widened with fear, but she wouldn't fight him.

She nodded her head.

"Why?" He demanded, narrowing his eyes at her. "I don't want you to hurt me." She whispered softly.

"Someone who has intended to hurt you, will hurt you regardless of whether you will fight them or not, Myra."

"Are you going to hurt me?" She asked softly. He looked into her wide eyes, narrowing his eyes at her again. "Perhaps... in the future." He answered, clenching his jaw. She released a shaky breath. "Well then, I must deserve it."

He turned away from her, unable to take her innocent eyes gazing up at him like that. He was even angrier now, how could a woman like her affect him, he didn't even know her. For all he knows she's putting up a facade.

He knew that wasn't true.

He had met many women, they all had a similar cunning gleam in their eyes and sly smile on their face. She didn't, he had yet to see her smile. She was very reserved and behaved like a proper, disciplined young woman. She was transparent and good as they come.

With that thought in his mind he closed his eyes and attempted to fall asleep.

-----------------------Here's the next part! Which most of you probably read already.

Sorry about the delay, I've been feeling a little bit down for the past few days. I think I'll probably cry myself to sleep, everything just feels really overwhelming.

Anyways, let me know what you think of this one.

Please Vote, Comment and Share.

Z.A.B

chapter 12

"Myra." He called, watching her sit up on the bed. "Yes Sir?" She answered gazing up at him. Her eyes always held gentleness within them, something he wasn't used to.

"Are you coming down for Dinner?" He asked, making his tone softer. "Oh..." she muttered, taken aback by his question. She was used to strict orders and demands, even from him. She nodded in response sliding on her high heels, following him down.

Her stomach rumbled at the smell that lingered in the air. She hoped it tasted as good as it smelled, it had been so long since she'd had something to satisfy her cravings.

"Hope pizza is okay." He said settling down. Myra settled down opposite him, unable to hide her excitement. "Yes!"

His eyes snapped up to her face and noticed the excitement in hers. He kept his face blank and pushed the box towards her. She looked up at him questioningly. "Aren't you going to eat?" She asked shyly.

"Ladies first." He nodded. She pulled out a slice and watched him take one too. She waited for him to take his bite first, not wanting to seem too eager.

Vincent pulled his phone out, pretending to be busy so the atmosphere doesn't fill with awkwardness, but it seemed impossible. He waited for her to finish her first slice before asking her anything.

He looked up at her too see her licking some sauce off her lip, he looked away quickly not wanting his mind to go into the gutter. After she had eaten it , he looked at her for a moment before deciding to ask her more questions.

"Myra."

She looked up at him, swallowing her bite. She cleared her throat awkwardly. "Yes?"

"Tell me about your relationship with Ben."

He watched her face drop at mentioning her husband. "There's not much to tell." She mumbled, putting her slice down.

She peeked up at him through her lashes. "I'm sorry. I'll tell you whatever you want to know."

Her heart throbbed wildly in her chest, afraid that he would lose his temper again. "Tell me why you've never been intimate with him." He stated. He'd been curious since last night, but wasn't sure on how to approach her apart from asking her directly.

"I- I think he doesn't find me attractive."

Vincent knew that was bullshit.

"Are you lying to me?" He asked, unable to keep the harshness out of his voice. She shook her head, her embarrassment increasing.

"He said I need to lose weight." She whispered, crossing her arms self-consciously, he could see her visibly shrinking in attempt to hide her body.

Myra felt her eyes watering again. "And?" He pushed, trying to get more answers.

"I went on a diet. I tried to make him h-happy." She continued after a second. A tear escaped from her eyes and she stood up from her stool, trying to rush past him to get away, but he was faster. He pulled her back into himself, she pushed his arm off her waist, but he only held her tighter.

"You're going to tell me everything. From the beginning to the end. Understood?" He growled angrily. Myra felt the same fear pulsing through her veins as she did on the first day. She nodded, sobbing softly. He let go of her when he was sure she wouldn't run away again.

"Can I p-please have a m-minute?" She pleaded, as tears continued to roll down her cheeks. He nodded.

She took deep breaths, grabbing some tissues and wiping her face before sitting down again.

He waited patiently, pulling out some drinks from the fridge unsure of whether she drinks or not.

She looked up at him after a few minutes and sighed.

"I only met him once before we got married. I said he will only touch me if I want him and we agreed on it. I did everything he asked me to. He said I needed to lose weight so before we went to those parties. I thought maybe if I was obedient, he would be a little nicer... accept me as his wife..." she said quietly, leaving out some details.

He stayed quiet after hearing it.

"Do you like him?" He asked.

Myra shrugged. "I don't know. I did try to get him to like me, I gave up. I just did what I was told."

"Why did you marry him?"

She bit her lip and watched him carefully.

"My parents thought it was a good match."

"So they forced you?" He asked, his eyes darkening. "No!" She panicked.

He raised his eyebrow at her, making her look down again. "Financially... it's been hard. I didn't want to feel like a burden on them so I agreed."

"How much did he borrow? I-if I may know..." she asked hesitantly.

"One million."

Myra's mouth dropped open. She couldn't believe it. What did he want to do with so much money.

"Do you know why?" She asked again.

"That's not my problem. The deal was he pays it back."

Myra nodded, averting her gaze.

He had enough answers for now. "Finish eating." He nodded pointedly. She shook her head, crossing her arms. "I'm done." She lied, moving to get off the stool.

"Myra." He warned and she stopped, keeping her eyes on the table. "At least finish your slice."

She released another breath, nodding slightly. She picked up her slice and ate it in small bites.

"I noticed you didn't bring your phone." He said.

"I don't have one." She answered with a shrug. He paused what he was doing and looked up at her. He didn't say anything else and waited for her to finish. He saw her eyeing the coke can, but didn't move to get it.

He waited a few minutes before pretending to be busy on his phone and opening the can and taking a few gulps.

He slid the can over to her and gave her a look. She bit her lip, hesitantly grabbing the can and taking a few small gulps.

She closed the box and put it in the fridge and washed her hands. She turned back around and watched as he stood up and walked up to his room. She followed him quietly.

Vincent walked straight into the bathroom and Myra quickly changed her clothes in his bedroom. As she finished, she heard Vincent coming back. She went to the bathroom and brushed her teeth and washed her face with cold water before drying it. She went and laid down on his bed, keeping to her side. He laid down staring at the back of her head. He was so tempted to reach out touch her body.

Vincent was unable to believe that Ben didn't even feel the temptation to touch her. However, that would mean he would touch her even if Myra didn't want it. That thought alone angered him. He wasn't sure how much longer he could control himself, but he knew no matter what, he would never force himself on her or anyone else. The t-shirts that she wore to sleep were short and tight, which would usually ride up and bare her stomach. Even now her shirt exposed a part of her waist. He clenched his jaw tightly, facing the ceiling.

Myra wasn't sure what to think about their earlier conversation. She was hoping he wasn't thinking badly of her. If she knew her future would turn out to be like this, nothing could have convinced her to marry Ben, not even her parents. She was just glad Vincent hadn't done anything so far.

Okay guys,

I've been gone for some time and I'm sorry :(

I will try to update from this week onwards. I'll update each book as I get to it. I'm securing a job at the moment and I'm sooooo excited to finally work. My whole family has been in quarantine for longer than you guys can imagine. We have a family wedding coming up and rules are so freaking strict and tests are so expensive. There is a teeny tiny chance that we can go, but it seems highly unlikely and I am sad. So you know what, anyone who broke COVID rules. Fuck you. I'm not sorry at all.

Anyways, let me know what you think.

Please remember to Vote, Comment and Share!!!

Z.A.B

chapter 13

Myra stared at the bland food in front of her. She peeked up at Vincent and Sam who seemed to enjoy whatever they were given. "May I be excused?" She asked looking at Vincent. He could not understand how she still managed to be so polite to him. He nodded and Myra quickly stood up and took her plate to the kitchen, wrapping her leftovers up and putting them in the fridge.

She was starving, all she wanted was some spicy pasta, but they hardly seasoned their food. She even doubted they had any chilli powder, or even heard of such a thing. She was already in bed, curled up on her side and quickly closed her eyes as soon as she heard him walk in. Dinner was a little later today; both men were out and about all day and came home at 9pm. Vincent went to his cupboard and pulled out his clothes to sleep in, which was usually just a pair of boxers and a sleeveless vest.

Myra sighed sadly, she tried not to think about the fact that he would hurt her, or maybe kill her. She only hoped he would make it as painless as possible for her. It was not like it her fault that Ben borrowed so much money knowing that he won't be able to pay it back. How can people commit such stupidity?

She heard the door opening again and stayed still. Maybe she could sneak down once he falls asleep and make herself something spicy. Her stomach rumbled at the thought and hoped that he did not hear it. He was lying beside her, not caring about her personal space. He always slept in the centre of the bed, not leaving much space for her, but it was fine, once Myra falls asleep she wouldn't move until morning.

She waited about an hour for him to fall asleep before turning to look at him. He was gorgeous, even when he slept. He looked like a model. His lips were slightly parted making Myra bite her own. She shook her head at the sinful thoughts entering her mind and got out of bed quietly, making her way down to the kitchen.

She opened all the cupboards looking for any spices she could find. Her eyes widened at the different things they had inside, even back home she had basic spices, but he had his kitchen stocked up with so many different things.

She quickly pulled out a pot and filled it up with some water placing it on the stove and pulled out a packet of pasta.

"What are you doing?"

She jumped and turned around bracing herself against the counter. "I uh nothing?" She squeaked embarrassed. "I knew it. You don't like the food?" Asked Sam. She blushed shaking her head in response. He chuckled at her embarrassment. "Here, I'll show you where everything is."

He pointed at all the different cupboards, telling her where the cups, glasses, forks and knives are. "Was I too noisy?" She asked. "Nope. We are trained to be alert even when we're asleep." He shrugged. "Do you want some?" She asked quietly.

"If you can save some for tomorrow. Otherwise I'm good." He smiled. Myra nodded, making sure she makes a little bit extra. "I'm going to go back to bed. Goodnight Myra."

"Goodnight." She nodded as he walked back out. She bent over the counter, placing elbows on it, leaning over as she waited for the water to start boiling. Being tired and hungry was never a good combination for her.

Myra was more worried about Vincent than anyone else. He was unpredictable. Sam was just a few inches shorter than Vincent, but his body was broader, regardless she still found Vincent more intimidating. He never laughed or smiled unless he was trying to scare her. Sam at least apologised for what he had said and occasionally joked around with her.

As her thought process came to an end. She felt someone watching her.

She tensed up.

She turned around sharply, gulping audibly. He didn't say anything, yet his dark eyes intimidated her. He took slow purposeful steps towards her, stopping in front of her. He lifted his hand tangling them in her hair, pulling it sharply. She yelped with surprise, lifting her hands and placing them on his chest.

He placed his hands on her hips, lifting her on the counter, spreading her legs out and pulling her forwards roughly. He leaned down, moving her shirt off her neck, inhaling deeply.

She saw someone standing at the door again and looked up to see Sam with a worried look on his face. As soon as he caught her eyes he smirked at her, winked and left both of them in the kitchen.

"Why didn't you have dinner?" He asked, gripping her hips tightly.

"I wasn't h-hungry." She lied, hoping he wouldn't hurt her. He bit her neck, making her jump with shock again. "Try again."

"I don't like the food." She said quietly, closing her eyes tightly. She expecting another painful bite, but this time he kissed her where he bit her, sliding his tongue over before pulling her skin into his mouth. She shivered, feeling her body cover in goosebumps at the intensity. She moaned softly, tensing her legs around waist pulling him even closer.

He pulled away from her neck, resting his forehead against hers, centimetres from her lips. He grunted annoyed, pulling away from her completely. She panted softly, unable to look at him.

She slowly slid off the counter, turning the stove off and putting the unopened pack of pasta away. "I didn't stop you from eating Myra." He muttered leaning again the breakfast counter. She stood still, feeling confused by his behaviour, he made it seem that he was angry at her.

He sighed when she didn't move to turn the stove on and walked back over to her. He turned the stove back on and pulled the pasta back out. "I thought you were mad at me." She said confused. He caged her between himself and the counter again, leaning down looking into her eyes. "I'm not angry. Quite the opposite actually." He stated as she continued to look confused.

"Oh?"

"You want to know?" He asked leaning closer, she bit her lip and nodded. She kept her eyes on his as they gazed down intently.

"I want to bend you over the counter and fuck you." Her eyes widened more than ever as a intense blush heated her face as her lips parted. He chuckled again, enjoying her reaction.

"Then why don't you?"

His head snapped up, his laughter quickly dying in his throat. Had the circumstances been different, he wouldn't have thought another second and bent her over. She was his prisoner and she wouldn't stop him just for that reason.

"I'm a killer, not a rapist." He laughed, only this time there was no trace of humour in his laugh. His dark eyes trailed over her face, before grabbing the pack of pasta and ripping it open. He poured it into the boiling water and added some salt and oil, while she stood there just watching him.

"What else do you need?" He asked as he grabbed a wooden spoon. "Are you going to answer me or do I have to spank you with the spoon?" He threatened taking a step closer to her again. She shook her head quickly covering her backside with her hands. "Double cream." She answered shakily. Once he turned away from her, he smiled at her reaction once again.

"And?" He asked returning with the cream. "Chilli powder, chilli flakes, chicken stock, black pepper and fresh green chillies." She listed and watched as he silently pulled out small glass jars of the different spices.

"Now?"

"Now wait for the Pasta to finish cooking." He nodded and stood in front of her, crossing his arms. She fidgeted nervously under his intense gaze, unsure of what to say to him.

She turned around stirring the pasta to make sure it doesn't stick together. More time passed in silence and the pasta only needed a few more minutes. She opened the cupboards looking for the strainer, placing it in the sink.

Vincent came over beside her, pulling on the heatproof gloves waiting for her to tell him. "I can do it." She mumbled, but he paid her no attention and picked up the steaming pot in his hands tilted it over the strainer.

"Wait!" She gasped. "What?" He asked panicked. "Don't throw away all the water.." She ordered and looked up at him to see him rolling his eyes at her. "That's enough." She said and shook the strainer a few times before pouring the pasta back in and opening the double cream and pouring it over the pasta. She grabbed the spices, generously adding the into the pot before stirring it together.

He silently pulled out a plate and spoon since it was extra saucy and placed it on the counter beside her. "Thank you Sir." She said glancing up at him.

She let it cook for a few more seconds and then poured it into her plate, walking over to the breakfast counter and settling down quickly. She blew over her first bite as her mouth watered.

Myra opened her mouth moving the spoon towards her lips and suddenly a hand grabbed hers. She couldn't help the angry look that took over her face as he quickly leaned forwards. "Don't!" She shouted, but it was too late. He chewed for a second and then his eyes widened as his face started turning red. He swallowed the rest before running over to the sink and rinsing his mouth.

Myra ran towards the fridge pulling out the cold milk and handing it to him. "It will make it better." He snatched the bottle from her and gulped it down. It wasn't going to take immediate affect but it soothed the burning sensation more than water. "How the fuck can you eat that?" He panted, taking another swig of the milk.

She bit her lip and turned around hiding her face. She clapped her hand over her mouth trying to stop the laugh that was threatening to bubble out of her. If she looked at him for one more second she would've laughed in his face.

"Myra?" He called confused. She took a deep breath before replying "Yes?"

He narrowed his eyes at her and grabbed her elbow, turning her around. Her brown eyes glittered with tears as she attempted to control herself. For a moment he thought she was upset, but then he looked down at her lips which she was still biting as a smile threatened to break through.

"You're laughing at me?" He asked bewildered. She shook her head desperately backing away. She couldn't take it any more as she laughed loudly, almost wheezing as she doubled over.

He stared at her as tears ran down her face, he had finally seen her laugh for the first time. Her smile was contagious and he could feel his own smile forming. He shook his head at her grinning at her.

"I-I'm sorry." She wheezed holding her hand up. "It wasn't that funny." He complained crossing his arms.

She nodded half-heartedly, taking a deep breath to control herself. Her stomach was aching that's how hard she laughed. She walked back over to her chair still grinning. Her food was still warm, perfect to start eating straight away.

He sat down opposite her, leaning his head on his hand. "Why's that so funny?" He asked.

"Please don't make me answer that." She said her smile dropping.

"Do tell." He urged curiously.

"Well... it's just that... someone fearsome as you, can't handle some spice. And your face was funny too" She added quickly, biting her lip.

He stared at her for a moment. "I suppose so." He muttered. She finally took a bite of her food and moaned at the different flavours exploding in her mouth. He leaned his head on the table while she ate. Her moans were the sexiest sound he'd ever heard and it nothing to help the current hard-on he was sporting.

She finished eating and walked over to the sink washing her dishes and putting the left overs in the fridge. She yawned sleepily patting her full stomach. "Let's head upstairs before you pass out in the kitchen." He teased, smirking at her as she blushed.

She followed him up the stairs into his room where she laid down straight away and closed her eyes. She sat up quickly and rushed to the bathroom. "What is it?" He asked concerned.

"I forgot to brush my teeth." She mumbled embarrassed, not making any eye contact. He sighed rubbing his hand over his face. He laid down on the bed and closed his eyes.

After ten minutes or so she came back out and laid down beside him, staring at his face. She blushed at his handsome features.

"Take a picture. It will last longer." He said with his eyes closed. She gasped, immediately flustered and shuffled away from him, but he quickly pulled her back against himself. Myra blushed even more once she was pressed up against him so intimately. "Goodnight." He whispered in her ear, smirking when she shivered a little.

She just closed her eyes concentrating on falling asleep.

----------------2.07.21

Heyyyy. I know this is a long chapter, but too short to be split up. I hope you guys like it.

Writing scenes like this makes being single even harder .

Unless a handsome guy wants to kidnap and romance me. I'm kidding!

And that Pasta recipe is legit and my favourite quick food recipe. I think they call it heavy cream in America. If you can't take spice like Vincent then reduce it!

How'd you find this one?

I ended up flying out to the wedding. I'm loving it

Please don't forget to Vote, Comment and Share.

Z.A.B

chapter 14

He hadn't touched her again, but she could always feel him watching her so intently, but when she turned around he would look away. It was already dark outside and he would be home any minute now. She sat down on his bed, wrapping her arms around herself.

After their moment in the kitchen he became much colder towards her. He slept further away from her too now. It was just confusing for her.

He had even started coming home later than usual, still at a fixed time and no matter how much she tried to sleep without him, she just couldn't. She wasn't sure if it was fear, or something else.

He stumbled in through the door, holding a bottle of whisky. "You're drunk?" She gasped. If he had been holding back before, the alcohol in his system would only boost his lack of control. "Myra." He slurred, sitting down next to her. She shuffled away from him, but he grabbed her hand pulling her beside himself. "Don't hurt me." She whimpered softly, staying still beside him.

"I wouldn't hurt you." He frowned, letting go of her hand. "You're so beautiful." He whispered, his grey eyes seeming darker than usual. She blushed, looking down at her lap.

He pressed his hand on the side of her face, pulling her face towards himself. "Kiss me, Myra." He demanded, pulling away from her. She looked up at him with wide eyes, shaking her head. "You're drunk." She answered, trying to put him off. "So why don't you come and take advantage of me. Kiss me." He smirked.

She looked at his dark eyes before, dropping her eyes to his lips. She leaned up to him, but he was too tall, she moved away blushing. Vincent caught on and slouched down slightly, leaning forwards again. Myra leaned forwards too, but paused when they were just an inch away from each other.

She breathed out slightly, before closing her eyes and leaning forwards, until she felt his warm lips against hers. She felt her face heat up instantly and her stomach tingling wildly, quickly pulling away from him. She didn't even feel anything when she kissed her husband on her wedding day. She opened her eyes, looking up at him shyly.

His dark eyes were focused on her plump lips, already wanting more. He leaned forwards again, grabbing the back of her head, pressing his lips against hers again. He pulled her lip between his, grazing his teeth over it gently, making her gasp. He didn't waste another second before deepening the kiss, slowly pressing his tongue into her warm mouth. Myra moaned against his mouth, leaning up and pushing herself into his lap.

She felt hot all over, her heart throbbed wildly in her chest and her hands felt slightly sweaty, she pressed them on his shoulder. He wrapped his other arm around her waist pulling her closer so she straddled his lap. He rubbed his tongue over hers, making her moan again.

He pressed her down into his lap, making her gasp. She felt him pressing against her thigh, making her jerk back. "It's okay, Myra." He whispered, letting go of her neck to adjust his erection, brushing her clothed center by accident. He placed his hand on her thigh, trailing up, gently squeezing her ass.

Myra felt herself freeze up and jumped off his lap, taking a few steps away from him. She was a married woman, making out with the person that's keeping her hostage. "Get over here." He demanded lowly, watching her tremble. She shook her head, feeling guilty. "Lie down, Myra." He grunted, standing up.

She gasped quietly, before obeying him unwillingly. She laid down in the middle of the bed, keeping hands beside her head. Vincent pulled his clothes off, throwing them on the floor lazily. He climbed on the bed, leaning over her, before placing his head on her chest and wrapping an arm over her stomach. "Your heart is beating so fast. Are you scared?" He asked, closing his eyes.

"Yes." She whispered shakily, feeling awkward. He pushed his leg under the blanket, jerking it up, before grabbing it and pulling it over both of them. "I won't hurt you, Myra." He whispered before drifting off. She felt awkward laying down underneath him, her hands were beside her head, and Vincent was laying beside her, but kept his head on her chest and held her close. She slowly brought her hands down, placing them beside herself, before closing her eyes.

Vincent woke up the next morning on an empty bed, groaning at the pounding in his head. His eyes snapped to the door as Myra stepped in looking at the floor. She held a tray in her hand, with a full glass of water and painkillers. She came forward, placing it on his side table. He stared at her, noticing the blush on her cheeks, she fiddled with her dress before turning around to leave.

"Myra." He called, narrowing his eyes at her. "Yes." She said turning around, but looking at the floor. He tapped the bed, signalling for her to sit down next to her again. She say down stiffly on the edge of the bed, playing with the front of her dress. He sat up leaning against the headboard, taking the pills and downing them with the glass of water.

"Did something happen?" He asked. Myra's eyes widened for a moment, he doesn't remember anything. "You told me to kiss you." She mumbled, causing her face to heat up more than it already was. "Did you?" He asked, shuffling closer to her. She nodded hesitantly, feeling his breath on her neck. He couldn't believe it, he would've thought she would run for her life. His mouth watered at the sight of her bare neck, he wanted to mark her, brushing his lips over sensitive neck and hearing her gasp.

He licked her neck, before sucking it hungrily. She leaned back against him, closing her eyes and biting her lip to hold back a moan. He rolled her over himself, pushing her down on the bed. She gasped pushing him off herself, but he pressed her hands into the bed. "You didn't run last night." He stated holding her down and leaning down, pressing his lips to hers again.

She didn't respond at first, making him pull back for a moment. She panted softly, looking up at him feeling unsure about what they were doing. He leaned down again, biting her lip and sucking it into his mouth. She moaned softly, only encouraging him to continue what he was doing.

He slid his tongue into her mouth, rubbing it against hers. He let go of her hands slowly, checking if she would push him away again. He pulled away again, she looked so sexy, panting and flushed. "Open your mouth." He demanded, his voice heavy with lust. She shook her head defiantly, immediately embarrassed again.

"Open it and stick your tongue out." She looked at him, wanting to tell him to stop, but couldn't get the words out. She wanted to obey him so badly.

She parted her soft pink lips, sticking her tongue out slightly. "More Myra." He grunted, almost impatient. He leaned down again, rubbing the tip of his over hers, before sucking it into his mouth, making her moan loudly. Her stomach tingled and spread her legs out, feeling lust wash over her body. She tangled her fingers in his dark curls, arching her body into his, feeling his naked chest pressed against her clothed one. His hard on was straining against his boxers, begging to be touched, but he didn't want to scare her away.

He pulled away from her, sitting up and staring down at her. She took deep breaths to calm her heart and fill her lungs with oxygen that he managed to suck out of her. She trailed her eyes over his torso, toned chest and hard abs. She bit her lip as she looked at his plump ones before looking at his face. He smirked down at the young woman spread out on his bed.

"Enjoying the view?" He asked, chuckling as she quickly looked away from him a deep blush coloring her cheeks.

Dayum, it's getting hot in here.

What do you guys think will happen next? Is she going to give in? Will Vincent get his money back and send her back to Ben?

Do you think it's moving too fast?

I really love the comments you guys leave even though there aren't that many. I still appreciate it.

Anyways please Vote, Comment and Share.

Z.A.B

chapter 15

A/N: violence

It had been weeks since their last kiss, Myra avoided him like the plague. She had just prepared dinner and walked up the stairs to call him down. She made sure she made something more edible for Vincent separately and something spicy for herself and Sam.

She slowly approached the door lifting her hand to knock, but froze. His next words made her blood run cold.

"Don't fucking test me Ben. I'll fucking kill both of you. Get me my money, or die." He threatened before cutting the call and throwing his phone on the bed. Myra felt like she was about to pass out. He was going to kill her. He flung the door open, glaring down at Myra.

Panic arose in her body and she ran from him. Vincent cursed loudly and rushed after her. She ran straight for the front door, pulling the handle down and opening it. He pulled her back roughly. "Sam!" He roared loudly. He walked out of his bedroom slowly, staying by his door.

"Yes Boss." He answered blankly. "Lock all the fucking doors and from now on they will always stay locked." He ordered, pushing Myra back towards the stairs. "Sam, please help me. He'll kill me." She sobbed, fighting his grip. Sam watched helplessly, he couldn't go against his orders. Sam ignored her pleas and glared at Vincent, before going to his room and slamming the door shut.

She ripped her arm out of his grip somehow. "Sam! Please." She cried out, running after him and managing to hit his door. Vincent grabbed her wrist, jerking her forwards roughly before bending down and throwing her over his shoulder.

She continued to cry and scream, hitting his back hard. He grunted in pain, she was really strong and he was only human, of course her constant punches were going to hurt him. He dropped her on his bed, before locking the door.

She crawled off the bed, feeling her legs give out from underneath her. She pressed herself against the wall, pulling her knees to her chest, wrapping her arms around her head, sobbing loudly.

Watching her run from him released the beast inside him. Vincent wanted blood. His anger had overpowered his senses. He pulled his gun out, rushing towards her. Her head snapped up as she heard him approach, screaming when she saw the gun in his hand.

He grabbed her hair pulling her forwards roughly onto her knees. She let out another scream of fear and pain, her scalp was burning from the intense pull.

Myra was struggling to breathe as she continued to panic, she closed her eyes tightly. He pressed the cold muzzle against her forehead causing her to whimper as she waited.

He glared down at her, watching as tears rolled down her face, her hair was a tangled mess and she continued to sob. She was waiting for him to kill her. She wasn't even pleading for her life, she had accepted her fate.

"Look at me." He demanded roughly. She opened her eyes and looked up at him, but saw the gun pressing against her forehead. His eyes met hers. All he could see was pain and fear.

He turned his head away and closed his eyes, her lifeless eyes flashed in his mind.

"Fuck." He growled, he slowly withdrew his hand and stood there for a moment, realising what he had done and was about to do.

He clutched his gun angrily and backed out of the room hurriedly, slamming the door shut. She sobbed loudly, staying on her knees, but as soon as she tried to stand up she felt nauseous. Black spots appeared in front of her eyes and she collapsed on the floor, passing out.

Vincent left his house, sitting down in his car and ordered his driver to take him as far as possible. He couldn't go back to his own house. He texted Sam to check on Myra, but received no reply to confirm he'd seen it. He knew he fucked up.

Sam checked his messages after an hour, but once he read it he rushed up the stairs and knocked on the door, but there was no response. He opened the door and looked inside only to see her sprawled out beside the bed. He cursed quickly rushing in and lifting her up and placing her on the bed.

"Myra. Open you eyes sweetheart." He called gently. He felt a strange protectiveness for her, nothing romantic though. He'd only threatened her because he had no choice at that time. He can't disobey Vincent on certain things, yet he didn't expect his friend to hurt her either. She was a good woman. He walked to the bathroom, wetting his hand before sprinkling it on her face.

A frown marred her forehead as she slowly opened her eyes completely confused. "Sam?" What-?"

Tears filled her eyes again and she pushed Sam as hard as possible. "Myra. I won't hurt you." He said softly not to frighten her. "No! No." She whimpered, climbing off the bed. She ran towards the bathroom, but Sam caught her as she struggled in his arms.

"Myra." He whispered as she sobbed. He wrapped his arms around her protectively, rubbing her back soothingly. She slumped onto him, pressing her face into his chest and cried. "He was going to shoot me. He wants to kill me."

"He won't. It's okay, he's not coming back." He consolidated. "Sam, p-please just k-kill me. I can't take this torture. P-please." She begged.

"No Myra. Don't be stupid. He won't kill you, neither will I." He whispered.

She continued to mumble incoherently, begging for her life, yet at the same time asking him to end it. Fear had made her irrational, she'd never seen a gun and seeing it so close made her realise she was seconds away from death.

He had been so calm the first few weeks and all of a sudden he pulled a gun on her. She passed out again, as her knees gave out underneath her. He quickly tightened his arms around her, pulling her on the bed again and tucking her in.

He pulled his phone out to see a string of texts from Vincent, to which he responded with one word; 'Bastard'.

She remained restless. Every time she started falling asleep, Vincent's cold glare and gun appeared in behind her closed eyes and she would jerk awake.

Vincent stayed in his office in one of the many homes that he owned, staring out of the window. His night was as restless as hers. All he could hear were her screams, see her tears as he held a gun to her forehead.

He felt as though a part of him had become weak, he'd killed women without hesitation, but he had to remind himself that Myra was innocent. He leaned back and closed his eyes, remembering the day he cooked and she told him what to do. That was the first time he'd ever felt some sort peace in his cold heart.

Myra clutched the blanket tightly, biting her lip to keep in any sobs. She feared he was going to walk in any minute. That he would shoot her when she wasn't looking. She kept her eyes glued to the door. Usually she'd already be asleep by the time he arrived and he would leave by the time she'd wake up. The only time they saw each other was at Dinner time, that is if he came on time.

Where one part of her was scared, the other part of her was hurt. After everything they did together she began to take a liking in him. She let herself believe that he wasn't a monster that he showed everyone.

But he treated her just like her husband did, as an object to show his power, although when her husband did it, it didn't hurt as much as what Vincent had done to her.

Eventually she was exhausted, she gave up fighting to stay awake and only prayed that she wouldn't have anymore nightmares for the rest of the early morning and hoped if that was the case, Sam wouldn't wake her. She just wanted to have some peace.

Don't hate me :((((((

I know a lot of you are going to hate Vincent, but he is a criminal at the end of the day. Let's see what he does next :/

How did you guys find this chapter. I know it's a little bit shorter than the other chapters.

Please Vote, Comment and Share.

Z.A.B

chapter 16

Myra remained on the edge although it had been a week. He hadn't come back yet. Vincent stayed away from his house for as long as he could, unable to look at Myra. He knew she feared him even more than before.

Myra was downstairs with Sam making Dinner after a whole week of staying in her room, only because he 'blackmailed' her to come out and help him cook because he didn't know how to. He could've easily called the chef in, but lied to her that he was unable to come due to sickness.

Despite being reluctant, she enjoyed cooking with him and momentarily forgot about Vincent. Sam noticed her sudden weight loss, she hadn't been eating properly and hoped if they made something that she liked she would sit and eat with him.

She sat down beside him while he poured spicy tomato and chicken pasta in two plates. "I'm not hungry." She frowned. "You're still eating." He ordered sternly, giving her a look that she couldn't argue with. She rolled her eyes at him and grabbed herself a fork and stabbed the piece of chicken.

They ate in silence, until Myra spoke up. "Do you know when he's coming back?"

Sam looked up at her with surprise, but shook his head. "I'd figure he'll be back soon. Very soon." He warned. She nodded plainly, unsure about how she felt, she knew for sure though that she was terrified of him. She didn't ask him anymore and decided to eat silently for now, the more she thought about him, the more her hunger seemed to dissipate. She tried to eat as much as possible, but only managed to eat half of what she had been served, but to be fair Sam had piled her plate more than his own.

She got up to wrap up her food, but not before receiving a disapproving look from Sam for not finishing her food. Myra scooped the rest of the food into a bowl and also refrigerated everything and began washing the dishes. "Myra, I'll wash them. Move." He demanded. "I'm already washing them." She answered turning to show her soapy hands and sponge. "Wash them."

"I said I am." She answered cheekily. "That's not what I meant." He muttered shaking his head at her. She shrugged and turned back around, continuing what she was already doing. Sam stood up placing his plate in the sink before, forming his hand into a cup and throwing water over her. "Sam!" She screeched, glaring up at him. "Aw, now you need to change your clothes." He smirked mockingly. If there was anything that Myra hated, it was wet clothes when she didn't intend to make them wet.

She rinsed her hands quickly, shoving him before turning around. She froze. Sam didn't seem to notice her hesitance. "S-Sam..." She whispered. He frowned, before turning around and looking at the exact spot that she was staring at.

Vincent.

He was back.

Myra clenched her fists to keep her hands from shaking, her breath had quickened a little as she gulped. Vincent stared at her intensely before turning his glare towards Sam. "Go up to your room, Myra." Sam demanded lowly. She took a shaky breath and looked up at him unsure, but he nodded at her reassuringly.

She looked down and walked past him, unable to keep herself from flinching when she got too close to him. She pulled out a simple maxi dress and hopped into the shower quickly, hoping he wouldn't be outside when she was finished.

She wrapped a towel around herself, drying herself before pulling the dress on, leaving the top few buttons undone. She hated collared dresses, they made her claustrophobic. Myra didn't know what to do with herself, part of her wanted to go downstairs and the other wanted to hide away. Although, she was curious about what would be talking about.

They wouldn't fight, would they? Obviously not, they wouldn't hurt their friendship, not because of her.

It seemed as if she waited for a long time for someone to come and get her, anxiousness settled over her.

She heard the door open and she froze, she already knew who it was without having to look. She turned around slowly looking up at him. He walked in further, closing the door behind himself, slowly walking towards her. Myra inhaled sharply, backing up every time he stepped closer. She knew there was no point getting away from him, he would have her where he wanted regardless.

She squeezed herself against the wall as he stopped right in front of her. "Myra." He breathed, she closed her eyes tightly turning her head away. He wrapped his arms around her waist, pulling her against his chest tightly. She whimpered with fear, keeping her hands by her side.

"Shh... I won't hurt you. I'm... I'm sorry." He whispered, brushing his hand over her back soothingly. He had never in his life apologised to anyone, even if he was wrong. The words felt so foreign on his tongue, but for her; he was ready to apologise as many times as she wanted to, until she accepted it. Myra felt tears filling her eyes and quickly was sobbing as she tried to pull away, but he wouldn't let her.

"Don't hurt me." She begged, continuing to struggle. He released her, stepping away from her, giving her some space. "I won't hurt you." He repeated. She shook her head, refusing to believe him. Myra slid along the wall dropping on her knees. "I know y-your going to kill me. S-so just d-do it."

He walked over to her, settling down on the floor opposite her. "I won't. I never intended to kill you since the first day. But when you ran...it was instinctive for me to react this way."

She leaned against the wall, wiping her tears only for more to roll down. "I know you're just saying that. When the n-next few weeks are over. I- I will die." She sobbed.

"You won't." He said gently. "But you-"

"Myra. I was threatening your husband. He is the one that borrowed money, not you."

She shook her head unable to believe a word he was saying. "Myra." He said softly.

She looked up at him hesitantly, he stared at her with a pained look on his face. How could he make it look so believable? His eyes trailed over her body, noticing her weight loss too. He sighed, shaking his head at himself.

"I won't hurt you. If I wanted to hurt you, don't you think I wouldn't have waited this long? I stopped on the first day when you told me to, does that mean nothing? I lost my temper speaking to Ben and then you ran away, almost ran out of my house. I lost control. I'm sorry Myra. I really am. I had never intended to hurt you. Never." He apologised again, pleading her with his eyes.

She took a shaky breath looking away from him. "I'm still scared." She whispered shakily. He nodded understandingly. "I won't touch you. I promise I won't hurt you either."

They sat there in silence for a couple of minutes until Vincent spoke up again. "Come on, sweetheart. It's time to sleep." They both stood up and Myra grabbed some clothes again, a t-shirt and sweatpants and changing her her clothes in the bathroom.

She laid down on her side again, pulling the blanket up to her chin. Instead of laying down with her, he went to the door. "Where are you going?" She blurted, feeling her face warm up again.

"I'm going to sleep in the other room." He stated, not looking at her.

"You don't have to sleep in the other room because of me." She muttered loud enough for him to hear. "I don't want you to feel uncomfortable."

She bit her lip and said nothing else, giving him one last look before turning to face the other way. He stood there contemplating for a minute and then walked towards the bed settling down on his side of the bed for the first time. Myra noticed that he kept his distance and was somewhat glad, she wasn't sure how she would react to his proximity.

He pulled his side of the blanket up his chest, closing his eyes. Neither of then said anything else and went to sleep, keeping their distance from each other, until she trusted him again.

Here is the next part my lovely readers!

He's finally back! Do you think his apology was enough? Also, I don't want to put warnings on any chapters anymore. I think it ruins the surprise or anticipation of what will happen next. I think that if you do get triggered by certain things, or are sensitive to some topics then please don't read this book.

Please read the note I made on my profile.

Hope you enjoyed this chapter.

Please Vote, Comment and Share.

Z.A.B

chapter 17

M yra sat on the porch alone, wrapping her arms around herself. They'd left her completely alone without a warning. Vincent had kept true to his promise and stayed away from her, but she didn't think he'd leave her like that. Even Sam wasn't here. What surprised her the most was the fact that they didn't lock any of the doors, hence why she was sitting outside in the cold.

Vincent had kept his distance from her, but there was something different, he was... more friendly. He had only been back for two days and then he left. He continued to convince her during the couple of days he spent with her that he won't kill her, or even hurt her. She was glad she didn't have any nightmares either. Myra did notice that she slept better with him in bed with him, even though part of her was afraid of him.

She missed both of them. It had been three days since she'd seen them last and neither of them contacted her at all. It scared her. What if something happened to them?

"Please come inside Ma'am, it's getting colder." Said the Maid gently. Now that she mentioned it, Myra shivered and nodded, rubbing her bare arms.

As soon as she stepped inside she was embraced by warmth and walked up to their room sadly, dropping herself on his bed clumsily. Why couldn't he just tell her?

She hated being alone now, before, she was used to it. When she lived with her parents, there would always be some sort of noise, whether it was arguing or obnoxious laughter. When she moved with Ben, she had to be quiet and proper, make sure Dinner was ready and everything was clean and tidy. Perhaps he did only marry her so he wouldn't have to pay for a maid, it made her feel like 1800 wife.

Yet he had 50k to pay her parents. Vincent never expected her to do anything like that, even though he had the power to make her do whatever he wanted. Sure she dressed well, but it was a set routine. She had to wake up early, even earlier than her husband; shower, dress up nicely, do her hair and a little make up before having to go down and make him breakfast and bringing it up to his room.

She wasn't sure how long she laid there lost in her own mind, thinking about her past, her family. She snapped out of her thoughts, hearing birds chirping outside now. It was early morning now and another night passed without any words from Vincent.

She closed her eyes, drifting in and out of sleep. She suddenly jerked awake, heart racing, eyes adjusting to the light shining into her room.

She was sure she shut the light and the door before she laid down. She rubbed her eyes, rolling out of bed, walking over barefooted. She stepped in and saw him.

But that's not what shocked her, it was the fresh stain on his shirt. He was sitting at the edge of the bathtub, holding a first aid kit. Her heart was beating out of rhythm as she went closer. She reminded herself that this is not the time to have a weak heart.

She trembled as she lifted her hands to unbutton his shirt. Her eyes welled up with tears as one traitorous tear rolled down her cheek. Vincent immediately caught it, wiping it with his thumb. "Don't cry Myra." He whispered softly. She pushed the shirt off his shoulders baring his toned injured chest.

"I... tell me what to do." She said sniffling softly, staring at the bleeding wound. "I can do it, you can go back to bed." He said shaking his head at her. "Please, Sir." She pleaded. He sighed, before speaking.

"Grab some tissue, by some I mean lots."

Myra rushed over to grab a new roll of toilet paper, wrapping it around her hand generously, before pressing it over the wound. "Harder." He demanded softly. She applied more pressure and he nodded. She watched as blood seeped through the tissue and raised her alarmed eyes to his. "It's okay, grab more." He nodded, replacing her hand with hers as she rolled more tissue, more than before and pressed it over the his wound again, applying more pressure, keeping her hand still.

"I like your dress." He complimented, letting his eyes trail over her body, it reached a few inches below her plump backside. He let his fingers trail over the ruched material, sliding his hand lower, until he reached her bare thigh. She swallowed nervously, keeping her eyes on his wound. "Any reason you're wearing such a scandalous dress?"

She blushed brightly, shaking her head.

"I wonder if your panties are just as scandalous." He teased.

"Sir please..." she pouted adorably, trying to hide her blush. He smirked up at her squeezing her thigh hard, making her gasp. Now was not the time to get distracted by the tingles she felt, or the warmth of his large hand stroking her thigh lazily.

The blood didn't seep through this time, and she hoped that it had stopped, but didn't move it just to make sure.

His hand didn't stop there, he slid it higher under her dress, reaching the top of her thigh. "Where is Sam?" She asked. "He went to see his girlfriend." He answered.

"Is he injured too?" She questioned looking up at him with concern. "A little." He nodded. She nodded biting her lip. She waited another five minutes before gently removing the bloody tissues. She threw the rubbish in the bin and grabbed a towel, making it wet with warm water.

Vincent watched her as she completely focused on wiping his chest gently, making sure not to get too close to the wound. He slowly moved his hand away, allowing her to bandage him up. "Is that okay?"

He nodded, not bothering to check it.

She moved away as he stood up to his full height, which meant she had to crane her neck to look up at him. "Thanks sweetheart. Let's get into bed." He suggested, urging her out. While her back was turned he unbuttoned his pants, pushing them down letting them drop on the floor.

"Do you mind sleeping on the other side of the bed for the next few days?"

She looked confused for a moment and then nodded quickly. Myra quickly piled the pillows up for him so that he wasn't completely flat on the bed. Vincent settled down stiffly, trying not to move his body too much. She noticed him reaching for the blanket and quickly grabbed it before he could. She didn't want the wound to open again.

She pulled the blanket up to his chest, tucking him in gently and sat kneeled beside him on the bed. "Do you need anything else?" She asked gently. He nodded in response.

"What is it?"

"You." He stated and watched as heat blossomed up on her cheeks.

"Oh..."

She looked down at her lap, realising that her lap was almost completely naked. He reached up, cupping her face in his hand, feeling his heart beat a little faster when she leaned into his touch. He leaned up a little but she pressed his hand on his bare chest shaking her head. "Stop moving." She scolded, narrowing her beautiful eyes at him. "Then kiss me." He smirked, and watched as she leaned over him.

She pressed her hand beside his head to balance herself and the other over the right side of his bare chest. Myra was a couple of inches from his face now. He kept his striking grey eyes locked with hers as she blushed. She licked her lips and bit down on her bottom lip. Vincent's eyes dropped to her plump pink lips, before looking back up at her eyes.

She leaned down further, missing his lips completely, pressing her face on his shoulder and laying down beside him. "You're such a tease Myra." He growled after all that anticipation. She giggled, pulling the blanket over herself. "Come closer." He demanded, pushing his arm under body, cupping her ass, pulling her against his side tightly. She gasped as she felt his bare legs against hers.

He slapped her butt lightly, chuckling when she squeaked with embarrassment. "Ow." She muttered, pouting and sitting up again. "I want a goodnight kiss."

"Not yet." She said shaking her head at him. "Myra." He grunted. She laid down again, keeping her head on his shoulder, placing her hand on his hard stomach and pushing her leg over his. He lifted his head slightly and kissed the top of her head, she smiled, closing her eyes. He would wait as long as she wanted him to.

Here is the next part, let's hope I have the motivation to write the next chapters.

Also I'm going to STOP putting warnings at the beginning of chapters, I just think it ruins the surprise of what might happen. Please read at your own risk .

Oh and if anything is medically incorrect I'm sorry. I tried using Google .

I hope this was alright, let's see what happens next.

Please Vote, Comment and Share.

Z.A.B

chapter 18

Vincent was now completely healed with the help of Myra, her constant care, nagging and restriction of movement. She forbade him from leaving the house unless it was an emergency and any meetings he needed to hold were to be held at home.

Usually Vincent never cared and even if someone of medical background would advise him to stay home, he didn't listen, but Myra would look up at him with those big brown eyes, silently pleading him to stay at home and he had no choice but to comply.

She had him wrapped around her finger, but she doesn't realise it. Even if she did, she wasn't the type of person to take advantage of someone's trust and Vincent knew that, which is why he left her home alone. He knew she wouldn't leave even though she had the chance.

Vincent wrapped a towel around his waist and stepped out of the bathroom into his bedroom, rummaging through his cupboard, looking for pants and boxers. He frowned, if he was staying home he might as well wear something comfortable rather than staying fully suited. He pulled out grey sweatpants and a white tank top.

He tied the sweatpants around his hips. "Vincent?" She called softly. He froze, he thought that perhaps he imagined it, but he turned around sharply. She tensed immediately at his sudden movement looking down. "I-I'm sorry Sir. It slipped." She apologised taking a step back.

"Say it again." He ordered and seemed to shy away even more from him. "I'm sorry." She repeated shakily. "No Myra. My name. Say my name."

Myra blushed looking up at him, her breath getting caught in her throat. His hair was still dripping, she watched as a drop slid down his chest over his strong stomach, soaking into the band of his sweatpants. She snapped out of her trance and looked up to see him gazing at her with a heated look. She shook her head.

Vincent walked towards her and she stepped back, her back now pressed against the door. "Say it Myra." He whispered as he leant down, holding her chin between his fingers. She gazed up at him, biting her lip before taking a shaky breath. "Vincent." She said again softly.

"Fuck." He growled. He leaned down further, brushing his lips against hers, smiling a little when she moved closer. She stood up on her tiptoes, wrapping her arms around his neck pulling down firmly. Vincent groaned against her lips bending down and lifting her up. She pulled with shock. "I'll fall." She panicked, wrapping her legs around him.

"Oh fuck, you're slipping Myra." He warned and suddenly let of her, causing her to release a short scream. She bounced on the bed and glared up at him. "You're such a..."

"Such a what?" He smirked leaning further down on her.

"...such a meanie." She pouted when she couldn't think of anything else to say. He chuckled lowly pressing her into the mattress. He grabbed her thighs, pulling them apart and settling between them on his knees. She was glad she was wearing something more loose and flowy, otherwise her dress would've ridden up higher.

"You're not leaving this bedroom until I say so." He demanded leaning over her. She blushed in response unsure of how to answer him without seeming too eager for what he was planning to do to her.

He pressed his lips against hers again after what seemed ages. She responded with the same eagerness, parting he lips for him. Vincent didn't waste another second, pressing his hot tongue into her mouth, sliding it over hers. She moaned against his mouth, trailing her warm hands over his strong biceps, squeezing slightly and feelings his tense muscles.

Myra tried her best to keep up with him, she tilted her head slightly, pressing her tongue into his mouth. Vincent slowed down a little as she shyly explored his mouth. He trailed his hand up her stomach, cupping her breast making her gasp with surprise. Myra's whole body tingled, subconsciously rubbing her lower half against his body.

He pulled away from her sweet lips, pressing wet kisses down her neck and over her the top of her breasts. She panted, squeezing her eyes shut tightly, having never felt someone touch her so intimately. "I'm going to take your dress off Myra." He whispered softly, her heart raced as she looked at him. He could feel her nervousness as she gave him the slightest nod to continue.

He pushed his hand underneath her, pulling the zipper down slowly. "I won't hurt you." He mumbled against her shoulder, pulling the sleeve of her dress down her arm. He sat up, using both his hands, sliding the dress down her arms further, revealing her breasts cupped in a simple black bra, then her stomach down to her hips. Eventually he pulled it all the way off, kneeling between her legs again as she crossed her arms across her chest and pulled her knees together.

She was utter perfection in his eyes. She met his eyes briefly, quickly looking to the side as a hot blush covered her cheeks. He curved his hands around her calves, pulling them apart gently, then gliding his hands up to her waist, squeezing it. As his hands caressed her, she felt insecure all of a sudden. She was sure he had seen women that were prettier than her and most likely thinner too.

"So beautiful." He smiled softly. He would never understand what those simple words did for her.

Myra arched into his touch as he gently caressed her bare skin. He leaned down, kissing her neck and sucking it into his mouth. Myra moaned surprised, she never thought her neck was this sensitive. It made her squirm underneath him. She rubbed her herself against him unintentionally, tangling her fingers into his hair, pushing him closer.

He continued marking his way down to the curve of her breast, biting her soft flesh. "Vincent..." she breathed softly. "Mmm, I love how you say my name." He groaned lowly. She felt embarrassed again and bit her lip.

"Pull your bra cup down for me Myra." He said gently. She gasped, shaking her head. "Do it." He ordered, looking down at her intensely. His grey eyes were much darker, swirling with lust as he watched her gulp nervously, slowly lifting her hand and hooking it into the strap of her bra and pulling it down her arm. He bit his lip hard as she revealed more of her sun-kissed skin.

She stopped for mere, the intensity of his stare made her feel hotter than she already felt. Vincent waited patiently, leaning down again, kissing the exposed skin. Myra hooked her fingers into her bra, pulling the cup down. Vincent groaned against her sensitive skin, causing her to moan again. Her skin tasted heavenly, he licked her dark nipple, pulling it between his lips and sucking it into his warm mouth.

Myra felt her panties dampening, even more than they were already. She felt a sharp tingle shoot through her stomach, ending right between her legs. Vincent used his other hand pulling her leg over his back, adjusting his hips so he was perfectly aligned between her legs.

He sucked harder and groaned as she lifted her hips, rubbing herself on him. She moaned louder at the sudden friction she felt between her legs, but she couldn't stop herself from wanting to feel it again. It felt as if she had no control over her body anymore, mindlessly grinding against his erection. Vincent pulled away panting harshly, gazing up at Myra who seemed to be lost in pleasure.

It was the sexiest sight he had ever seen, her soft pink lips remained parted and she moaned and gasped, her eyes were shut tightly and her back was arching into, pressing her breasts further into his face.

He could feel the heat between her legs every time she pushed up into him, he was throbbing with need. He was sure she was wet enough to leave a patch over his sweatpants. He quickly turned his attention to her other breast, pulling the cup down and latching on to her nipple again, hearing her moan again, causing him to twitch in his pants.

She now had both legs wrapped around his hips as he rotated his hips in a slow rhythm, meeting her hips every time.

"Fuck Myra, you're killing me." He groaned pulling away from her breast.

"Vincent." She moaned, digging her fingers into his shoulders. He grabbed both her arms, pinning them into the pillow under her head, pulling away from her. She panted opening her eyes, confused.

She attempted to tug her hands out of his grip, but his grip only tightened.

"Are you wet for me, Myra?" He asked, his voice deeper than usual. She shook her head, both of them knew she was lying. He smirked down at her. "Open."

She glanced at the two fingers he held out in front her. Hesitantly, she parted her lips enough for him to push his fingers in. "Suck."

She shook her head. "Myra." He warned, narrowing his eyes at her. She whimpered softly, sliding her tongue over his fingers and hollowing her cheeks, sucking them deeper into her mouth. Once he was satisfied he pulled them out and watched as she panted.

"Myra, you know you can stop me right?" He asked gently, tracing a wet path down the centre of her stomach. She gave him a nod. "I'm j-just nervous." She mumbled self-consciously. "It's okay. If it doesn't feel right, then tell me."

She nodded again, holding her breath as she felt fingers tease the edge of her matching cotton underwear, before slowly dipping in, curving over her mound. His touch was so light, yet it tickled her. He finally dipped his fingers between her folds, sliding over her hot wet slit. "You're so wet, Myra." He stated with a teasing smirk playing at his lips.

She looked away bashfully, closing her eyes as he began circling her clit. She bit her lip hard as she felt a hot tingle burning between her legs. Myra was already sensitive, but she wanted the ache between her legs disappear. Vincent rubbed her slowly, letting her get used to the feeling, before sliding his fingers down to her entrance, nudging her gently.

She opened her eyes wide looking up at him, but not saying anything to him.

As he slowly pressed his middle finger in, she grabbed his wrist out of panic. "Vince..." she panted nervously. "Do you want me to stop?" He asked, pausing. She took a few breaths, before shaking her head in response. She didn't move her hand as she felt him move again. He felt her soft, wet heat wrap around the tip of his finger as he inched it in deeper into her.

She winced, squirming against his hands to get used to the feeling of him inside her. He was knuckle deep inside her now. He held still for a moment, knowing that this was the first time anyone touched her so intimately. "Does it hurt?" He asked concerned, his eyes looking over her face. "A little." She answered embarrassed.

He pressed him thumb over her sensitive clit, slowly rubbing it. She bit her lip as she felt tingles, spread all the way to her toes, causing her to tense pleasurably.

He slowly started pushing in and out of her, feeling her relax slightly.

Myra moaned, as her walls fluttered around his fingers. He pressed his thumb harder over her clit, massaging it as he fingered her slowly.

He sped up a little and her moans and gasps increased. She wrapped her arms around his neck, pulling him down on herself.

She felt hot, her breath was coming out in pants now. She could feel the knot forming in her stomach, causing her to tense more than before.

"You gonna cum for me, sweetheart?" He whispered and she whimpered, nodding her head against his shoulder.

"Good girl. Cum for me." He groaned going faster. He could feel her pulse and tighten even more, until she moaned his name loudly, biting his shoulder releasing around his finger, hard.

He continued, but slowed down a little more. She continued to whimper and moan softly, but Vincent had other plans. He was going to get one more orgasm out of her sweet body. Already sensitive, began moving his fingers again. "Vincent, what..-" She panted, looking up at him.

"One more, Myra. I want one more from you."

She shook her head, but subconsciously thrust her hips against his hand. He began doing the same as before, only this time he was faster, his hand was drenched from her wetness. His finger slid in and out of her with ease as he continued to pleasure her.

Her feet dug into the mattress below her as she lifted her hips, tensing up. Myra felt breathless, light headed, but she didn't want him to stop.

"Just like that. Fuck." He grunted. She panted, feeling herself tighten again. She fisted her pillow hard, body shaking with the intensity of her next orgasm. "Good girl." He praised as she tightened hard and came again.

He slowly withdrew from her body, slid his fingers over her slit. "Stop." She panted, grabbing his wrist again. He chuckled, leaning down and catching her lips in a kiss.

"Are you okay?" He asked against lips. She nodded blushing fiercely. He hummed and pulled away from her.

He fixed her bra straps, pulling her cups back up. He got off the bed, grabbing a shirt for her and dressing her up gently. "Let's get you cleaned." He urged, pulling her off the bed. Her legs felt like Jelly as she took a step. Vincent wrapped his arm around her waist, walking her over to the bathroom and she sat on the edge of the bathtub. "Take your panties off."

"What? Why?" She asked pressing her legs together. "Maybe because I want to bend you over the bathtub and..." he paused, giving her a dirty smirk. She blushed again, shaking her head. He pulled out a small towel, making sure to dampen it slightly before he walking over to her.

Myra stood up, hooking her fingers into the band of her underwear, pushing them down until they fell on the floor. She widened her legs her slightly as he came over and wrapped an arm around her waist, holding her steady.

He wiped her gently, until he was satisfied. Myra looked down as he moved the towel away to see a little bit of blood and another substance smeared together.

She bit down on her lip hard, feeling guilt settle in her stomach. Everything they did together felt so good. Her husband held her hand when they were in public, but she never felt the same warmth and tingles she felt with Vincent. She shouldn't feel guilty, Ben knew what was going to happen to her, or why Vincent took her.

"Are you alright Myra?" He asked gently, realising that she was lost in her thoughts, frowning slightly. Her eyes snapped up to his. "Yes." She nodded.

"Did it feel good?" He questioned, throwing the towel in the laundry basket. She nodded shyly, looking down. "I'm glad your first orgasm felt good. Hopefully the next few are better." He smirked.

"It wasn't my first." She blurted, before smacking a hand over her mouth. She looked up to his eyes darken with anger, soon glaring at her. "You said Ben didn't-"

"It wasn't Ben." She said quickly, averting her gaze.

"Who was it? An old lover of yours?" He grit out. She looked up at him hurt. "I didn't lie when I said no one else touched me."

"Then-..." he paused, his eyes widening with realisation before grinning down at her. "You touched yourself?" He asked surprised.

The blush on her cheeks gave him his answer. She refused to look up his, crossing her arms self-consciously. "Answer me." He said, placing a finger under her chin so she looked up at him. She gulped nervously. "Yes."

Her answer was so quiet, he almost didn't hear it. "How often?" He asked as he thought about the sweet, innocent woman, naked, in bed, with her legs spread out, pleasuring herself. He felt like he would combust in his pants just imagining it.

"Just once." She whispered.

"I'm going to need a live demonstration." He demanded playfully, smirking at her wide eyed look. She shook her head, denying him immediately.

"One day Myra, I'm going to claim every single inch of your body and you will let me. Won't you?" He said in a deep husky voice that made Myra shiver and nod hypnotically.

He pulled away from her, pulling his sweatpants down. "What are you doing?!" She squealed, turning away. "I'm going to shower again, so unless you want to watch, you can wait downstairs or in our room." He smirked. "I-I'm sorry that I can't... didn't-" she stuttered embarrassed.

"I can take care of myself. All I need to do is imagine you in my bed, touching yourself while you're waiting for me to come home and fuck you." He whispered into her ear, feeling her shudder against him. She pulled away from him, glancing up at him as his eyes trailed over her body appreciatively. She bit her lip bashfully, before quickly leaving him in the bathroom.

Myra sat on his bed clenching her thighs, it was as if she could feel his finger still, yet at the same time she felt empty. Shaking her head, she quickly changed her clothes, pulling out a black dress with short sleeves and matching black pumps.

"Myra." He groaned as soon as he stepped out of the bathroom. "Yes?" She asked confused.

"Stop looking so sexy. There was not point of me showering." He grunted.

"Stop looking then." She stated as he glared at her. She bit back a smile. Vincent ripped off his towel, chuckling when she squeaked and covered her eyes.

"You're so annoying." She mumbled, turning around and waiting for him to wear something.

After a few minutes, she felt him wrap his arms around her waist, pulling her back against his hard chest. "Are you sore?" He asked with concern.

She did feel a little awkward between her legs and her nipples would sting ever so slightly whenever her bra shifted. "A little." She said quietly.

"Hmm. Maybe I should kiss it better." He suggested lowly. She quickly shook her head, her legs still felt a little shaky.

"I'm hungry." She said quickly, in an attempt to change the topic. "Mmm, me too. I know exactly what I want for Dinner." He said, letting his hand trail down the side of her body. She jumped away from him, not even looking back before hurriedly walking out of the room. "Come back here!" He shouted. Myra giggled, trying to run downstairs as quick as possible.

Vincent chuckled following her down, she was quite fast for someone that wore heels. She walked into the kitchen to see Sam sitting at the table already eating. He gave her a once over, smirking knowingly. "Someone had a fun evening."

Myra blushed shaking her head. "What? N-no."

"Maybe you should've looked in the mirror before you left." He laughed, pointing at the love bites. She gasped, covering her neck immediately. Just as she turned around to leave, she bumped into Vincent. He held her biceps, pushing her backwards, but she hid her face against his chest.

She felt extremely shy, unable to look at either of them. "What's wrong Myra?" He asked gently. She mumbled something against his chest and he frowned, before glaring at Sam who continued to grin. "What?" He asked again.

He bent down slightly in an attempt to hear her. "You left marks on me?" She asked quietly, so quiet that Vincent almost didn't hear again.

"Is that why you're hiding?" He grinned, matching Sam's expression. She didn't answer at all. Vincent couldn't help but find her adorable, it made his heart race slightly.

"Myra sweetheart, come on, let's eat." He said prying her off, but she shook her head. "I thought you were hungry?" Again she shook her head in response.

"You know what I want to eat." He said, laughing as she let out a whine of embarrassment. "Okay. I'm sorry. No one will say anything. Right?" He said looking at Sam pointedly. "For now." He snickered.

He pushed her back again, this time she moved back but kept her face down. He tilted her face up to see her cheeks coloured in a rosy hue, biting her bottom lip. Unable to help himself, he leaned down kissing her gently.

He pulled away to see her blushing even more, looking up at him with wide brown eyes. "Vincent..." she murmured. He smiled down at her, taking a hold of her hand and pulling her towards the table.

They both sat down. Vincent sighed as she made no move to filling her plate up. He served her the lasagna and then put some in for himself too. After a few minutes, she finally picked up her cutlery and began eating, still blushing but feeling a lot calmer than before.

Soon they were all laughing together, both of them careful not to embarrass her for the remainder of the night.

I think this was the chapter that made me decide to write a book on them. Well there you finally have some sexy stuff. It gets a little awkward writing scenes like this, because uhm... author who's sexually frustrated all the time.

Hope you liked the chapter and get ready for what will happen next.

Please Vote, Comment and Share.

Z.A.B

chapter 19

Myra and Vincent grew closer as the days flowed by. Every night before they slept, they usually would have a heavy make out session before curling up in each others arms and falling in to blissful sleep. She enjoyed every second of it. Vincent never demanded anything more than she wanted to do. Myra felt eventually he would get tired of waiting and find someone else, but one look from him told her that he only wanted her, even if he didn't say the words.

The more time they spent together, the less guilty she felt about being married. Part of her wished that she met him earlier, then maybe there would have been a chance that she would've been happier.

She had been waiting for Vincent to come to his room, but he hadn't come to see her all day so she decided that she would go to his office. She walked to his office, her heels clicking softly on the way.

She couldn't help the butterflies swarming in her stomach. He made her too nervous too function normally sometimes. She knocked on the door of his office and heard him respond. She opened the door and stepped in, her heart rate accelerating as she saw him sitting at his table with Sam opposite him.

She blushed knowing that Sam would probably make fun of her. She bit her lip and looked at Vincent who was busy trailing his eyes over her body before meeting her eyes. She gulped at the heated look in his eyes.

"Well I guess it's time for me to leave." Said Sam standing up and giving Myra a smirk.

She gave him a sarcastic smile and responded. "Yes it is." Both men enjoyed her wit, she was finally opening up to both of them, not fearing them anymore.

"Have fun." He said walking past her and then stopped giving her another playful smirk. "And remember to use protection."

Myra gasped loudly and shoved Sam who threw his head back and laughed on his way out. He shut the door and Myra fidgeted nervously now that she was alone with him. "Come here." He ordered and Myra obeyed walking up to his side. He stood up and grabbed her elbow and pulled her against the table.

He gripped her chin gently tilting her head backwards, kissing her heatedly. Myra wrapped her arms around him as he lifted her onto the table. He pushed her dress up making it roll over her hips. He large hands stroked her thighs and Myra felt heat blossom in her stomach. She gulped and spread her legs nervously.

He stepped between her legs, cupping her backside and pulling her closer to himself. She moaned against his mouth and panted as he pulled away only to kiss down her neck.

"Are you wet, Myra?" He asked, knowing the answer already. "No." She breathed. He pulled away from her neck and watched her face as he trailed his fingers up her thigh, teasing the edge of her panties.

Vincent was already so hard, he had been holding back on his own release. He grabbed her hand, placing her hand on his bulge and watched her eyes open wide.

He released her hand, but she didn't move it away, biting her lip shyly. His finger slid in from the side of her panties, immediately becoming soaked in her juices.

She rubbed her palm over the bulge, unsure of what else to do. "Unbutton me." He ordered, keeping his eyes on her face. He watched her cheeks flush again, but was looking for any signs of discomfort. He continued to slide his finger through her wet slit as he waited.

She brought her other hand to the top of his pants, unbuttoning it. She couldn't look up at him as she slowly pulled the zip down. Vincent pushed his pants down slightly baring his lower half. He grabbed her hand again, slowly sliding it down the top of his boxers. Myra's lips parted with surprise and kept her eyes on his crotch.

She gasped as her hand came in contact with his hot and hard length. He wrapped her hand around it firmly, then took a stepped even closer to her. He held back shudders of pleasure, he felt like he would crumble in seconds. There was something so incredibly hot about her innocence and the way she shyly explored him. He wanted to corrupt her.

He showed her how to move her hand along his length and then gently slid his finger into her making her gasp again. It felt so big against her hand, her fingers didn't wrap around it.

Myra moaned softly as he started moving his finger back and forth whilst rubbing his thumb on her clit.

Vincent pushed his boxers down, uncovering himself. Her eyes widened, it was huge, nothing compared to his finger. He pulled his finger out and moved her hand away closing the gap between their bodies.

She panted and gazed up at him fearfully. He clenched his jaw tightly, sliding the tip between her wet folds and groaning. Her words were stuck in her throat and she gripped the edge of the table, knowing that her nightmare was going to become a reality. She closed her eyes tightly as she felt him press firmly at her entrance. He pushed forwards and she whimpered. He dislodged himself, bumping the tip on her clit. She moaned again.

He grabbed her wrist again, placing her hand on his erection and two fingers on her clit. She opened her eyes, to see a scolding look on his face and she quickly averted her gaze again, realising he only did so to lubricate himself.

"I won't force you."

She was just about to apologise but he claimed her lips with a slow kiss, starting of gently before dominating her mouth. Her circled her clit and Myra began sliding her hand up and his length. Her blush deepened, she was using her own bodily substance to please him.

Myra's stomach tingled and her quickened her hand just as he circled her faster. She panted and moaned against his mouth. She grabbed the collar of his shirt with her free hand, tugging him closer, wrapping her legs around his hips. He groaned realising she was matching his pace.

"Vincent..." she moaned. He felt himself come closer and closer. Everything about her was sexy, her moans, the way she said his name and her voice.

Things were becoming too hot for both of them to handle. Myra dug her fingers into his chest, her breath becoming shorter, as well as concentrating on gripping him harder, sliding her hand faster. Just the thought of him being inside of her made her shudder. Vincent grunted lowly, thrusting his hips against her hand.

With loud moans, both of them released over each other. They panted loudly, catching their breaths. She looked up at him with a shy smile.

He cleaned her up and pulled her dress down again, then tucked himself back in buttoning up his trousers, before stepping away from her body.

"You're going home, Myra."

Well Um... don't hate me.

I trying to try out different ways to motivate myself to write and I think making notes on papers is helping. Just easier to ahead.

If you haven't read my note, then please check out a preview that I have posted of my next book 'The Wife" and let me know what you think.

Thanks for all the love.

Please remember to Vote, Comment and Share.

Z.A.B

chapter 20

Myra clutched the pillow to herself. He hadn't come back to his room again. He'd done it again. He had hurt her once more. How could he send her back to Ben after everything they had done together?

She just froze on his desk when he uttered those words without any emotion, right after they had touched each other so intimately.

How was it humanly possible to switch like that?

If he wanted to use her, then he should've just used her and not make her feel as if he wanted something more. She sniffled into her pillow, soaking it again with her tears. She shouldn't known he wouldn't want her, she was married afterall. How could she have imagined a future with him when she belonged to someone else?

As she sat there and cried, she realised that all of it was just her stupidity. She wished that she had been smarter, but he just made it seem too real. All she hoped was that he wouldn't come to see her at all. Part of her wanted to hit him as hard as she possibly could and another part of her wanted to beg him to keep her here and not send her back to that place, where she would be all alone again.

There was a soft knock at her door and she quickly wiped her tears, trying to put on a brave face.

"Myra?"

She immediately recognised Sam's voice and felt her lip quivering again with sadness. He had become an actual friend overtime.

He opened the door slowly and stepped in, shutting it gently. "Oh Myra." He said sympathetically as he walked closer to her. She sat up on her knees as he came towards her and quickly pulled her into a firm hug.

He rubbed her back soothingly as she continued to cry into his shirt. "Don't cry, Myra." but that only made it worse. He waited patiently, allowing her to release all her sadness before they started talking about anything.

After a long time Myra pulled away, her thighs ached from staying in the same position, but she couldn't get herself to care very much.

"Sorry I-"

"Don't be silly. Let's get comfortable."

They both shifted onto the bed, sitting up against the headboard side by side.

"Why are you so upset?" He asked. Myra frowned, if he didn't even know why then that meant she was definitely over reacting.

"It's nothing... It's stupid." She answered, shaking her head and clearing her throat.

"Tell me. It's not stupid if it's making you cry like a baby."

"I'm not a baby." she grumbled, feeling more tears filling her eyes.

"Then tell me." He insisted.

She remained silent for a moment, trying to gather up the courage to say the actual words.

"It's Vincent."

He scoffed, "I know that, love."

"He just... is like a switch. Some days he stays really close to me and other days like yesterday he pushes me away like I mean nothing to him."

"He's just like that Myra-"

"That doesnt give him the right to hurt anyone." She said sharply.

"You're right. I completely agree with you. He doesn't know how to manage his feelings towards you, which I think is really stupid. I mean after last time I thought he would have learned his lesson but no."

"He doesn't have feelings for me, Sam." she whispered brokenly. "No one does. My husband didn't think a second before handing me over to strangers who could've done whatever they wanted with me. How can I actually expect anything from someone who had taken me against my will?"

Sam listened quietly.

"I don't think I deserve to be wanted by anyone. If people were to somehow find out that I had an affair with my kidnapper, they would call me all types of names, to make it worse I'm married. It doesn't matter what my feelings were towards him, I shouldn't have done anything with him and was stupid enough to fall for his sweet words. Wherever I've been so far, nearly everyone has treated me like an object to use and abuse however they wanted."

She paused, tearing up again.

"I feel so broken and hurt by his actions. I just wished that I never agreed to Ben's proposal; that I never met any of them." she cried. Myra pulled her knees up to her chest and turned away from Sam, so that he wouldn't see how shattered she was. "They are both the same."

"I'm sorry Myra. I wish I could say anything that would make you feel better, but I know there is nothing." He whispered.

"Do you know when I'm leaving?" She asked softly

He hesitated.

"Tonight."

Myra didn't answer him and instead got up from the bed, pulling out her small suitcase and placing it on his bed. She held it together for the time being, not wanting to cry anymore until it was time for her to leave.

Sam sighed, unsure of whether to help her. She pulled out her dresses that she had brought with herself, leaving the expensive ones in there.

"Are you not taking those?" He asked, immediately regretting it.

"No. He can keep those for his next victim." She answered sourly, making him cringe. She eyed the short dress, before closing the cupboard. That was the last dress she had worn in the changing room where he had touched her so gently for the first time. She shook her head, removing that memory from her head for the time being.

He was not used to her harsh answers, but he was also not surprised, she had been through so much these past few months, it was understandable.

"I'm going to shower." she mumbled, taking out some clothes for herself and walking into the bathroom.

He was torn between both of them, but he knew for sure that he sided with Myra. He would not forgive his friend for making the same mistake again of hurting someone as innocent as her. She reminded him too much of his younger sister, someone who he had lost. Her death was the reason why he had joined Vincent, to take revenge and once he had taken it he never left.

He sighed. He didn't want her to go back to that monster.

Hey my amazing readers. I was at work today (just came home) and didn't really have much to do so I thought why not write a chapter while I'm doing nothing. I know it's really short, but I thought it's better than nothing.

If something doesn't make sense I'm sorry, I kept interrupted by my coworker who couldn't his business.

Let me know what you think.

Please Vote, Comment and Share.

Z.A.B

chapter 21

The night came faster than Myra anticipated and Sam had already brought her bag downstairs.

"It's time to go, Myra."

She bit her lip and looked around his home one last time. She could clearly remember the day she came in; frightened and fearing for her life and now she didn't want to leave.

Sam walked to the front door and opened it for her as he waited. Myra sniffled, putting her head down and leaving. They both walked to the car in silence and settled down.

"Myra..."

"Y-yes." She whispered softly, looking out the window.

"I'll come and get you, even when he doesn't. I'm not going let you stay with that rat." He promised angrily.

She smiled sadly, shaking her head. "It doesn't matter, Sam."

For the first time in her life she felt absolutely helpless, there was nothing she could do to save herself. She blamed herself for getting into this position, her parents had still given her a choice at the end of the day. She should've refused and then she wouldn't have ever met Ben or Vincent.

The drive back was silent, but halfway throughout it, Sam held her hand giving it a comforting squeeze.

"Thank you so much, Sam. I wish I had a brother like you." She whispered leaning her head against his shoulder.

"You remind me so much of my sister, Myra. She was just like you, sweet and innocent."

"What happened to her?" She asked softly.

Sam gulped, he'd never talked about it, except when he first came to Vincent.

"She was murdered, they had no reason. It was just pure malice. That's why I joined with Vincent. I killed those motherfuckers. I wish you weren't involved, because once you're in, there is no way out."

She gave his hand a comforting squeeze, unable to consolidate him with her words. It made her wonder what her fate would be?

They stayed quiet for the remainder of the journey. The closer she they were getting the more dread settled in her stomach, it was getting to the extent that she thought maybe she was going to throw up.

The tension in her mind continued to rise and she couldn't control it much longer. Tears ran down her face again as she thought about going back to Ben, to the person who didn't care about her at all.

"It will be okay. I know it. We'll be keeping an eye on you. "

She just nodded in agreement, her mind going back to Vincent again. She would've stopped if he even gave the smallest sign that he wanted her to stay. He didn't even say goodbye. He didn't even come to see her. How could he be so heartless at once.

The rest of their ride continued in silence, until they finally stopped outside her husband's home.

"Sam..."

"I know you don't want to go back. Be brave, I'll come and get you sooner than you will know."

"Promise?"

"I promise Myra, even if it gets me killed."

"I don't want anything to happen to you."

"And nothing will."

He hugged her one last time and pulled away, wiping her tears off her face with his hand.

"Come on."

The driver opened the door and she slowly stepped out of the expensive vehicle. Her suitcase was placed beside her and Sam came out standing a few feet in front of her. He walked towards the door and just in time Ben opened it.

She clutched the handle tightly and followed Sam, rolling her suitcase behind herself.

"You've got two weeks, Ben. After that, well you know what will happen."

Ben just nodded in response.

Sam grabbed her forearm tightly and she looked up gulping at his angry face, but she saw right through it. He gave her arm a gentle squeeze and pushed her forwards. It was his way of saying goodbye.

She did not know how, but she managed to hold her tears in for the time being. He climbed back down the steps and did not turn back again. She gulped down her emotions and closed as eyes tightly as the door of his car slammed shut.

"Myra..." said Ben weakly. She couldn't get herself look up at him. "I'm so sorry." He apologised, pulling her into a hug. She stayed still as he wrapped his arms around her. "Did he hurt you?" He asked cupping her face in both his hands. How could he act like this after everything he put her through?

"No." She answered shakily. "He didn't touch you...? Or force you?"

She gulped thinking of an answer to give to him.

"No. He- he said was going to wait until six months would be over..." she lied.

He didn't ask her anymore questions and pulled her into his home. She stepped inside after months, but it felt strange, as if she was a guest. There was no sense of belonging anymore. She should be happy, but she was lonely again. She hated it.

Ben continued to fuss around her, asking her if she needs anything or wants to eat, but she shook her head.

"I want... my own room." She requested, knowing that she wouldn't get what she asked for.

"Okay... you can move into one of the guest rooms, which ever you like more." He agreed. She looked up at him with some surprise, which he noticed.

"I know things between us were rough, but I want to work things through. And hopefully... we can be friends."

She gulped, but nodded. She knew she could never accept him as a friend, even if a certain grey-eyed man hadn't shown interest in her. She was lucky, that Vincent and Sam took care of her to some extent, more than what Ben had done being her husband.

"I want to rest." She mumbled, avoiding his eyes. He sighed but nodded. She walked up the stairs to one of the spare rooms, not caring much about size and looks. She just wanted to be alone. Ben pulled her small suitcase up to her new room.

"If you need anything, Myra, let me know."

She nodded again, avoiding eye-contact. She was surprised at his behaviour. If only he was like that at the start of their marriage, maybe she would've been happy with him. She did place her own conditions in front of him, but that did not mean he had to be so harsh towards her. Even just a friendship could've benefited their rough relationship. She heard the door click shut and sat down on the single bed, kicking her shoes off.

She thought about Vincent again and tears filled her eyes again. She shouldn't have allowed him to come so close to her. She laid down on the bed, unable to fall asleep without his arms around her waist. She tossed and turned but nothing helped. She wrapped the blanket around herself tightly and closed her eyes, only focusing on her breathing.

It was working. Her body relaxed as she forced herself not to think about anything but her breathing. She fell asleep, nuzzling into the warmth that the blanket provided her.

▫°•▫▫_____▫▫•°▫

Hey. I finally have an update for you guys. Its short but I feel there is nothing more than I could've added to it. I think there will be about 10 more chapters and it will be over. I am going to take another break then, because this break was so that I could focus on other things. I was still stressed af lol.

I told you guys about my Short Story being taken off, but I have uploaded some of them again, but they have their own books now, instead of being compiled in one Book. If you are interested then, feel free to have a look.

Anyways, I hope you guys enjoyed it. What do you guys think of Ben's behaviour?

And don't we just love Sam □

Thanks for reading.

Please Vote, Comment and Follow.

Z.A.B

Chapter 22

Myra's P.O.V

    I opened my eyes tiredly. It was exhausting to be thrown around like a toy. On top of all that, developing feelings for someone who does not care for you one bit. If they did care then they wouldn't leave me when I needed them the most.

Now I was back here, to do what I was brought here for. I got up from my bed and freshened up in the bathroom, dressing appropriately to how Ben liked it.

I did dress up when I lived with Vincent, but I guess the fact that he found me attractive reduced how insecure I felt wearing such dresses. I even noticed him staring, with that look in his grey eyes that had me heating up. I sighed sadly and pulled out whatever dress my hand touched first.

I brushed my fingers through my hair in an attempt to make my curls look neater, but there was no point until I showered and dried my hair properly and right now I couldn't be bothered.

I went down to the kitchen and prepared breakfast for him. I was back to cooking bland food. I guess a nice fatty burger could cheer me up momentarily, even Sam and Vincent had begun to enjoy seasoned food. I frowned at myself, I need to stop thinking about him. There's no way I would see him again. If Vincent was certain that he wasn't getting his money back, he would have never sent me back.

I guess it only proved that his wealth was more important than I was to him. Maybe he did just use me. I held no value in front of his money.

Whatever.

I served up the scrambled eggs on a plate and put them on a tray, ready to take them up to Ben's room, but as I poured the fresh juice into the glass, he walked in and sat down at the counter.

"Hey." He greeted.

"Morning." I answered, leaving out the surprise I felt from his unusual greeting.

"You don't have to do this anymore, Myra." He muttered somewhat guiltily.

I stared at him for a moment, noticing that his youthful look was deteriorating since the last time I saw him. He was stressed. I mean it was both of our lives at stake.

I decided to ignore him for now as I had already cooked the food, it would have been nicer if he told me last night instead.

I washed up the pots and spatulas that I used and cleaned everything until it was spotless before returning to my room. I had nothing else to do here.

It was even worse to have nothing to do, my mind would just wander off, thinking about him. It upset me how much he affected me. He was the only man that I actually allowed to get close to me. It was not like I lacked attention, but I knew most of them only wanted me because of their strange obsession with wanting to have women that were pure or untouched.

Yet it was the same men that took their 'virtue' or 'purity' and regarded them as used. I have seen it in my culture, which is why my Father was so protective of me, but he had also made the mistake. He had misread Ben. But how could I blame him, when I have made the same mistake with Vincent. He probably got off on the fact that no one had ever touched me.

There was no way that I was going to open up to him or any other man ever again. They are all the same.

I unpacked my suitcase since I had nothing better to do and stored my clothes on the hangers. I shoved the empty suitcase under the bed and sat down again. I tried not to think too much about it all, but I knew if I could go back in time I would never agree to this proposal, even if I got paid for it.

The rest of the day passed slowly. I could not wait for nightfall any longer and locked the door. I felt safer with the door locked. Maybe it was so save myself from another home invasion, God knows how many other people Ben had borrowed money from.

It was also nice to be alone, no one would see me cry or stop me from doing so. Ben knew better than coming to my room again. I honestly didn't even want to see his face for the next few days as I got over this trauma.

And I knew as much as I hated Vincent, I missed him. He was the reason I could not sleep alone anymore. I was so used to having his strong arms caging me against himself all night, making me feel wanted and safe.

I felt tears welling up in my eyes again, but I looked up at the ceiling, refusing to let them fall for someone who threw me out. He didn't care so why should I? Why should I waste my tears on him?

All these questions were useless. Tears slid down my face as my eyes could no longer hold them. I gave up and cried again. I managed to hold back all day, but now I was feeling it again. I was feeling lonely. I couldn't talk to anyone anymore.

The only friend I had was Sam and I had no way of contacting him. He was irreplaceable. Every time I thought about our first meeting it made me smile. He was just big friendly giant. That was the best way I could describe him. I felt stupid for even being scared of him in the first place.

He was the first one to comfort me. He confided in me too. I hope his friendship was genuine, otherwise I don't think I would be able to believe anyone.

I laid down in bed and closed my eyes, taking a deep breath and releasing it. Nothing can hurt me while I sleep. I pulled the duvet around myself tightly, closing my eyes and imagining it was 'him' with his arms around me.

I felt myself slowly dozing off, the warmth was comforting. Darkness was taking over gradually.

I jerked awake.

There was something in my room. It was buzzing loudly. I panicked and switched on the bedside lamp, looking around.

I focused on where the sound was coming from and it was from my bed. I got off it and listened closely. It was from underneath it, but the only thing under the bed was my suitcase.

I pulled it out, feeling the top of the suitcase until I felt a vibrating sensation against my hand. I unzipped the small pocket of the suitcase and pushed my hand inside it hesitantly.

My fingers met with cables and the vibration had already stopped. I pulled out the tangled mess. My mouth dropped open as I noticed the sleek device attached on one side and a portable charger on the other.

It vibrated again and the screen lit up with a number. It rang again for a few seconds before it stopped and came up with a notification. Maybe I picked up the wrong suitcase somehow, but I knew this is the one I took with me when I left this place.

I pushed the suitcase back under the bed and it rang again, making the faint buzzing sound.

I bit my lip and held device in my hands. Should I answer it? What if it was someone dangerous?

I took a deep breath as my heart pounded in my chest with nervousness.

I swiped the answer button and pressed the phone to my ear.

Silence. That's all there was.

I opened my mouth to speak, but my words got stuck in my throat.

"Myra..."

▫°•▫▫_____▫▫•°▫

Hey everyone.

I'm back with a short update but an update none the less. I hope you guys enjoy this one as I'm starting to work on the next chapter.

Also if anything is contradicting from what I have written in the beginnig, don't worry I will change it so the story flows more smoothly. Once it's finished, it will go through major editing since my grammar and punctuation suck, lol.

Please Vote and comment what you think. (Not edited)

Also check out my short stories. I feel like it's such a set back having to promote the other stories again and start from scratch, but I'm slowly getting there.

What short story should I work on next? I have 2 Vampire ones in mind, ones more dark than the other, but let me know. Thanks for the support

Lots of love,

Z.A.B

chapter 23

Myra's P.O.V

My eyes widened as his voice came through the phone.

"Myra... I-"

I pulled the phone away from my ear and cut the call. My heart was racing at the sound of his voice. He couldn't do this to me again. He's not allowed to hurt me like this.

The phone vibrated again, flashing with the number again and I tapped the red button again.

I bit my lip, even after sending me back, he won't leave me alone. What an idiot. A handsome idiot.

I guess it wouldn't hurt to annoy him a little, would it?

He rang it again and I answered it, pressing it to my ear.

"Myra-"

I cut it again, holding back a smile. It was the only thing that I could probably do right now to make him feel even a percent of what he had done to me.

Again, I answered the call and as soon as he spoke I cut the call. I had to admit, it was very entertaining.

I did it a few more times and then answered the call again.

"Myra." He growled lowly. His tone changed. He was angry.

"You don't get to be mad at me." I answered with as much attitude as possible, before ending the call again.

After messing with him a few more times, I answered the call and held the phone to my ear as I laid down.

"Myra." He whimpered. My heart. He sounded so defeated.

"What?" I asked sounding angry, but I could feel my voice wavering with emotion. The heartache was coming back, and the feelings of betrayal caused tears to fill my eyes again.

"I'm sorry... Myra." He apologised.

I sniffled, moving the phone away from my face. I didn't want him to hear me cry, I didn't want him to know how much he affected me.

"Please don't cry." He pleaded.

I bit my lip to hold back any sounds and took a deep breath.

"Why do you care?"

I knew it was obvious from my voice and he already heard me crying.

"I do care. You're the only person that has made these last few months tolerable. I just..."

"You mean by using me for your pleasure?" I accused.

"Fuck no, baby."

My stupid heart fluttered at the pet name. No. He couldn't just be sweet and sugary to convince me.

"You're lying." I mumbled.

"No, I'm not lying. You know I'm not a liar. I cherish the moments I spent with you. Fuck. You haven't even been gone for twenty-four hours, but it feels like it's been months." He confessed.

"Do you think I'll forgive you for saying a few sweet words to me?"

"I can only hope so, but I also know that I've hurt you too many times." He muttered.

"Why did you send me back?" I asked.

"He paid me half the amount. He said he would pay me the rest, but he wanted you back. I should getting the remaining amount in 2 weeks."

"And you weren't man enough to tell me everything yourself."

"No... no, I wasn't man enough. You- you unman me, make me weak. Even if you wouldn't have begged me to let you stay, all it would have taken is one single tear from your eyes and I would've killed him. I'm a man of my word, Myra, but you make me want to break every promise I've made."

I wiped my tears away, laying down on my side. His words were so heartfelt. I've never heard him struggle to explain himself like this. I didn't even know how to respond to him.

"Myra baby?"

"Hmm?" I responded.

"After he pays me back. I want you to leave him and come back to me."

"What if I don't want to see you?" I countered.

He was silent for a moment, obviously not expecting me to be so cold towards him.

"Then I will come and take you, by force."

I felt my breath get caught in my throat. Why did that sound so hot? I gulped down the excitement my body began to feel at his words.

"Whatever." I mumbled, clenching my legs together to stop the tingle.

There was a brief silence between both of us, neither of us talked. I could hear him breathing lightly.

"Are you tired?" He asked softly.

"Hmm."

"Okay. Goodnight."

I moved the phone away from my ear to cut it.

"Don't cut it." I heard him say faintly.

"Why?"

"I... I cannot sleep without you, but perhaps knowing you're on a call with me at night might help me."

"I should torment you." I stated.

"You have been since the day I laid my eyes on you." He said accusingly.

"I have done nothing to make you feel this way." I said a little harsher than I intended.

"You do not need to."

And that's where I left it. I didn't know whether to be happy or sad that he missed me, even though he hadn't said it. I guess I was happy that I had some way to contact him. But I was not going to give in so easily. I was going to make him beg for my forgiveness, maybe even use Ben to anger him even more. But there was a chance that that might be too dangerous. I almost forget that he is a criminal. A criminal that I like.

I heard his breathing slowing a little more, until I could feel that he fell asleep. I sighed and closed my eyes. At least I wasn't alone. At least I wasn't going to be here forever. After Vincent gets the rest of the money. I'm filing for a divorce and going back to my parents.

I had no where else to go and I know my parents will welcome me back without any questions, they know I don't give up easily. I don't want to tell them the details of what exactly went down, but I would assure them that Ben is as poor as us. I focused on his calming breaths before falling asleep, comfortably.

The End

□

°•□□_____□□•°□

I'm just kidding.

I'm not really sure of the interaction between both of them. I found it funny that she cut the call so many times.

I guess she should've been more upset. I just couldn't get myself to make her cry anymore. At least she knows she's his weakness. Anyways, is anyone else's wattpad glitching really badly, because mine was.

For my next story I'm planning to do a marriage one. Maybe enemies to lovers.

Another idea I had was a typical story, but it will be two books, probably quite short, maybe 15 chapters each. I'll post a short intro of each one when I have enough chapters.

What do you think will happen next? There's about 7ish chapters left. Who's excited for the ending.

Please remember to Vote, Comment and Share.

chapter 24

Myra's P.O.V

I opened my eyes the next day, stretching my limbs and moaning with satisfaction.

"Mmm. I love that sound."

I gasped and jumped simultaneously at the deep sound that rang through my room, blushing fiercely. His voice!

The phone!

I dug it out from under the duvet, I must've pressed a button whilst sleeping.

"You're still here?" I asked, surprised.

"Where else would I be, baby girl?"

I gulped, my stomach swarmed with butterflies at the sound of his voice.

"Well... you could be here, with me... we could be having fun..." I answered slowly, wondering if I could tease him.

"Don't, Myra. I'm already so hard." He groaned. I heard some shuffling.

"I'm about to have some fun... care to join me?" He asked suggestively. I could hear the smirk in his voice.

"W-What?" I stuttered weakly.

"I think you know what I mean, baby."

I gasped.

"No... I've never- I don't-"

I heard his deep chuckle over the phone and it tickled me right between my legs.

"I know you haven't done much. But if you're ever in the mood, I'm open to a hot, steamy, sexy phone call." He offered.

"I- I have to go!" I squeaked.

"Wait-"

But I didn't. I cut the call quickly, flushing with embarrassment and excitement. How is it possible for him to affect me so much just by talking, just by his voice?

Did I affect him like that?

I was quickly distracted from my thoughts when the phone dinged again.

It was a message from him.

'You're such a tease. I will take you, soon.'

It sounded threatening, but hot at the same time. There were several underlying meanings of his text, but I didn't want to think of them. I wouldn't be able to relieve myself, I felt too embarrassed to touch myself again. The first time I did it, it was kind of unintentional, I had no idea what I was really doing. One of my friends from college had told me about it and curiosity got the best of me. I'm glad I didn't do it again after that, otherwise I know I would've been addicted to the rush of pleasure that I felt when Vincent touched me there.

I shook my head and got up, freshening up in the bathroom. I brushed my teeth and washed my face with cold water, realising that I didn't really have anything to wash my face with except a soap bar. I stared at it for a moment, before digging around for something to half the bar with. One for washing my hands after using the toilet and the for washing my face until I had something proper.

Disgusting, I know. I just hope it doesn't make me break out.

I wasn't really sure about what else to do at this point. I hated staying in my room for too long. I liked my freedom there. I felt more freedom in my captors house rather than my husbands, but I guess it's time to accept that.

I made sure the phone was completely silent and put it on charge, hiding it under the mattress. It's unlikely that Ben would bother coming in here, all he knows is that Vincent mistreated me while I was there, but in reality he treated me better. I guess there were more positives than negatives, but each negative was a setback for our 'relationship'. I wasn't even sure if I could call it that.

I walked down straight to the kitchen, starving. I hadn't really eaten much since I'd arrived. I couldn't be bothered to make anything extravagant, I fried 2 eggs, sunny side up and two pieces of toasted bread. Fried eggs were probably one of the few things that tasted nice seasoned with only salt and pepper.

As I was lost in my thoughts, I was interrupted. "Myra." He said with a small smile. I didn't answer, but instead glanced at him letting him know that he had my attention.

It was strange seeing him smile at me. I don't ever recall him doing that ever.

"How are you feeling?" He asked, sounding genuinely concerned.

"Better, thank you." If only he knew why.

"That's great..." He mumbled, creating an awkward silence. I stopped eating for the time he was here with me.

"I know it's too late... I want things to work out between us. I'm sorry for everything. I know my apology means nothing at the moment, but I promise I'll make it up to you."

I was taken aback by his words. It was too late. I have been through so much because of him. And I was committed to someone else even if that person was not committed to me. Right now, I had no choice but to agree to his words. He looked sincere though he was unable to meet my eyes, but then looked up at me for my answer.

I nodded.

"I guess... I guess we can work something out." I mumbled, looking down at my plate. He stepped closer to me and leaned down and I froze. He kissed my cheek gently, before pulling away, giving me another small smile.

"We will go out in a couple of days and enjoy ourselves, okay?"

I nodded again.

"I'll see you later."

"Bye."

I stared down at my plate. He wanted nothing to do with me and now that I like someone else, he suddenly has feelings for me?

I was confused.

I finished my food and washed my dishes and went back up to my room, locking the door. I had a lot of time to fix my room and place everything where I wanted.

I took the phone out from under the mattress and checked it for any messages, but so far there were none. He was probably busy.

Just as that thought crossed my mind, the device lit up with a notification.

'Call me when you're free.'

I smiled immediately, but waited a little before calling him. I didn't want to seem desperate. I was going to torture him for as long as I'm here.

I went to the bathroom and looked at the items available for a shower, but there wasn't anything.

What kind of guestroom was this?

I decided to go to Ben's room and grab some of his spare items. He was not home yet, which was strange, he had a very strict routine. I shrugged and went into his room and took out a few necessary toiletries and even an expensive facewash and went back to my room.

I sighed and finished my shower, pulling on a plain oversized tshirt and made sure the door was locked before making myself comfortable in bed.

I took the phone and texted him.

'I'm free.'

I waited for his respond when it was instant.

'Call me.'

I made a face. I was not going call him.

'No.'

And as soon as I texted my reply he called me. I waited a few seconds before answering.

"Hello?"

"Hey baby."

"What have you been up to all day?"

"Nothing. I set my room up and showered." I responded.

"Hmm. Nothing interesting them?" He questioned.

"No- oh wait! Ben and I relaxed together." I lied.

He was silent for a minute.

"And?" His voice sounded deeper. I bit my lip for a moment, thinking about whether I should continue.

"He said that he wants to give out relationship another chance and then he..."

"He what, Myra?" He growled.

"He kissed me..." I knew that was a stretch.

"You better be joking, Myra. I might not do anything to you, but Ben is a whole other story."

I gulped. He might not hurt me?

"You're going to hurt me?" I squeaked, my heart was already pounding.

"Yes, but don't worry. I'll make sure you enjoy it."

My whole body heated up, knowing that whatever he meant was obviously sexual, but how could pain be pleasurable? It scared me a little.

"I- I was joking. He only kissed me on the cheek." I admitted panicking slightly.

"Are you giving him another chance?" He asked.

"No. Maybe if... circumstances were different... if all this wouldn't have happened." I said carefully.

"I would've had you one way or another." He promised.

I didn't know what to say in response, but I knew my body had its own reaction. The possessiveness in his voice helped me imagine his expression. His eyes are probably dark and narrowed and his face hard with anger and maybe jealousy.

He probably sensed my quietness and changed the topic to what he had done throughout the day.

"What are you wearing?" He asked out of the blue.

"A tshirt... why?" I asked confused.

"Just a tshirt?" He confirmed.

"Yes..."

"Fuck." He cursed.

I blushed again, as I do every time his voice turns lustful.

"Is your door locked?"

I swallowed again.

"Why?"

"Because I don't anyone to see what's mine. Understood?" He ordered possessively.

"Yes." I whispered.

The butterflies in my stomach became intense. What did he want from me?

"You're too tempting, Myra. I only need to hear your voice and I'm hard like horny fucking teenager."

"I... I don't know what to say." I managed to say.

"You don't need to say anything, baby. But maybe, you could take that shirt off."

"No!" I gasped and shook my head, knowing he can't see me.

"I need to see you. Right now."

I sat up with the phone held up to my ear. Would he come and get me?

I heard a strange beeping sound coming from the phone and looked it. It was a video call request. I slumped with disappointment.

"Accept it."

I looked at myself on the reflection of my phone to check if I looked okay. I pressed the button and his face popped up on the screen. I held the phone, facing it away from myself. I laid down and placed a spare pillow on the side and leant the phone against it, turning to the side.

He stared at me intently, smirking. I avoided looking at the phone, feeling too shy and embarrassed right then. I could feel his gaze even through the video. I grabbed the blanket, pulling it over myself up to my nose.

He narrowed his eyes at me. "Move it."

I shook my head.

He sighed, placing the phone on the side too and laid down... shirtless.

It felt uncomfortable at first, but he just talked to me, not expecting me to answer him much. He told me things about his childhood, happy memories, which were very few, but things changed as they got older. His life got a little better. He was telling me things he'd never told anyone. I wasn't sure how much time had passed, there was nothing on the video that could indicate anything.

I yawned, and at my failed attemp to hide it, he stopped.

"Go to sleep." He said softly.

I was about to argue, but he gave me a stern look.

"Leave the video on."

I pouted.

"Don't give me that look. I've seen you sleep before and I know you drool a little." He teased and I pulled the blanket over myself, embarrassed again. I didn't know I drooled!

His laugh rang around the room and I pulled my blanket down just to see him that moment.

"Goodnight, Myra." He said.

"Goodnight, Vincent." I mumbled.

He bit his lip, giving me that look, before shaking his head. He closed his eyes, a small smile adorning his face.

It took me some time, but I eventually fell asleep.

☐°•☐☐━━━━━━━━━━━━━━━━━━━━━☐☐•°☐

So, IDK about this chapter. I think it doesn't flow how I wanted it too, but oh well. I will edit it once it's complete.

I hope you guys enjoyed it!

Please Vote, Comment and Share.

Also check out other stories under my profile.

Lots of love,

Z.A.B

chapter 25

Everything was going fine between Vincent and I. The only downside was that I missed him very much. I craved being near him, to feel his arms around myself while I slept.

Ben hadn't really said much since then, I wondered where he would be, but didn't concern myself too much. He did say we were going to go somewhere, maybe he was too busy trying to find a way to pay Vincent the remaining amount of money.

I waited impatiently to retreat into my room for the night and call him. We were video calling every night since then, it was much better. He had also packed a pair of headphones in the suitcase and they were Bluetooth. I had never used any of these devices properly to know the functions and when he asked my why I hadn't used them I felt embarrassed. I didn't know how to connect them.

He pursed his lips at me and then gave me instructions on how to connect them together and then I could hear his even clearer than before. His voice was just... so incredibly deep.

He sounded so hot. Everything about him was attractive. Sometimes at night I'd wake up with the dim light shining on my face and I'd see him sleeping peacefully.

I wanted to text him so badly and tell him how much I missed him, but I didn't want to give in so quickly without any consequences for him.

It was around 6 o'clock in the evening and I had already gone to my room, since I had nothing else to do.

I sat down on my bed, staring at the phone, contemplating on whether I should message him.

A loud knock made me jump. I shoved the phone under my pillow and checked for any visible cables, but it was clear. I cleared my throat and opened the door.

"Hey." He smiled softly. His blue eyes glimmered with hope.

"Hi." I answered with not much emotion.

"I was wondering if... you would like to go out with me tonight." He asked nervously. He lifted his hand, holding a red rose. My lips parted with surprise, it wasn't much... but it was effort. I had to play along with him.

"I... yes. Thank you." I mumbled, taking the rose from him.

"Get ready and we will leave, okay?"

I nodded and smiled a little, he stood there for another moment and then shook his head and left. I closed the door and locked it, grabbing my phone again.

'Text me when you're free.'

I debated on whether to tell him that I was going out with Ben.

I responded with a 'Yes' and immediately the phone rang.

"I've been dying to hear your voice, Myra." He grumbled, making me smile. He sounded so cute when he is annoyed.

"Unfortunately, you won't hear it for too long today." I responded with a sigh.

"Why is that?"

"... Ben is taking me out today. On a date." I mumbled, unsure of what his response would be.

He stayed silent for a few seconds and I heard him exhale loudly.

"Where?"

"I don't know. But it will be later tonight."

"Take your phone with you." He demanded, sounding angry.

I frowned. "No."

"Myra. Don't fucking argue with me." He growled, and even over the phone the harshness of his voice made me flinch.

I didn't respond to him. I was taken aback by his tone.

"Fuck." He groaned.

"You can't talk to me this way. It's your fault that I'm even in this mess, again. You should've just ended everything when you had the chance!"

I cut the call and threw the phone on the bed, holding my head in my hands. Tears filled my eyes again, so much for missing him. The phone rang a few more times, but I ignored it. I would not talk to him until he changed the way he spoke to me. I'm done with everyone walking all over me. I didn't expect him to talk to me this way, especially after everything that's happened.

I felt like such a loser, I had spent majority of my life allowing everyone to take decisions for me and telling me what to do. If only I learned to trust my instincts, I would've saved myself from this crazy life and remained happy in my life of poverty. I sighed, wiping my tears and standing up.

I was going to tell Ben I wanted a divorce.

I want to get away from everything.

Tonight would be the perfect time. I already knew the date was going to be a drag, because nothing could make me forgive him for what he made me go through. It was over.

☐°•☐☐_____☐☐•°☐

I stared out the window as we drove to an undisclosed location. He had clearly downgraded his car too and was now driving himself instead of having a driver.

I put on a simple white dress that came up to my knees and left my hair untied. My curls looked better than usual and I didn't want to mess them up. The ride was silent, I thought maybe he would try to speak to me or talk about things, but he seemed silent.

Maybe he wanted to save it for the date. I sighed and leaned back in the seat, watching everything blur past us.

After another twenty minutes we slowed down and I looked outside. We were pulling into someone's driveway.

I got out of the car once it was parked, completely confused. I looked at Ben to see him already looking at me, he gave me a small smile.

"I just need to pick something up." He stated.

"I'll wait in the car then." I muttered opening the door again.

"No, no. Come inside." He insisted. I contemplated for a moment and then shut the door, walking towards him. We walked up to the door together and he rang the doorbell. I hated meeting new people. I was kind of glad the social parties were done forever.

The door opened, revealing a woman around her thirties. She was smiling, but I could tell it was not real. She wore a thick layer of make up, which looked orange on her complexion.

I pursed my lips as she ushered us in with a very high pitchen greeting. Part of me hoped that this would be a quick pick up of whatever Ben had to get, but my hopes were crushed as we entered their guest lounging area.

I looked up to see who the friend was and froze. His eyes were already on me before I even noticed him. I took a deep breath and stood close to Ben, hoping I could avoid him.

He walked up to us and greeted Ben, before turning his piercing eyes towards me, looking me up at down. I shuddered with disgust, but hoped it went unnoticed.

"I believe we haven't been introduced properly, I'm Frederick. It's nice to see you again, Myra."

He lifted his hand in front of me again and I stared at it, not wanting to touch him at all.

"Thank you." I answered politely, placing my hand in his. He brought it up to his mouth and kissed it before releasing it, quicker than last time.

He turned his attention to both of us.

"Please meet my fiance, Britney." He introduced, wrapping his arm around her slim waist and pulling her close.

I felt some kind of relief knowing that he had a fiance. He wouldn't act shamelessly in front of her, right?

"Please come and sit. Babe, why don't you grab some drinks?"

We settled down opposite each other as his fiance went and got some drinks. She balanced 4 champagne flutes and bottle champagne and brought them in, placing then on the table.

He popped the bottle open carefully and poured it in for his fiance and then turned to me.

"I'm sorry. I don't drink alcohol." I mumbled, embarrassed.

"Oh, of course not. I'll grab something else for you." He said getting up.

I sat silently as Ben and Britney made conversation about something uninteresting. He returned with a glass bottle of coca cola and a bottle opener. He held it away and popped it open and I watched it fizz.

"So Myra. How are things going with you?"

I turned to look at Britney and feigned a smile.

"Very well. Thank you. Congratulations on your engagement. When is the wedding?" I asked, smoothly.

"Oh! Not that soon. I have to do tons of shopping and contact an event organiser. I want it to be perfect." She gushed, looking at her fiance. He smiled and held her hand in his.

"Whatever you want, baby." Hs agreed.

I resisted making a face of disgust, they seemed so fake. Money and wealth is so important to them.

I picked up my glass and held it for a moment. I looked back at Frederick and he raised his glass a little and took a sip. I lifted my glass and took a slightly longer sip, enjoying the sweet taste of the soda.

I occasionally joined into their conversation, sipping and finishing my drink. After a while of sitting with them I felt a headache coming on.

"May I know where the bathroom is, please.?" I asked.

"Down the hall, 2nd left." He nodded, before looking back at the group.

I stood up and walked to the toilet, finding it quickly and locking it.

I felt a wave of dizziness wash over me and felt my heart sink. What was happening to me? My vision started to blur and it felt like it was too hot.

I closed the toilet lid and sat down on it, holding my head. I opened my eyes, but it was becoming more and more difficult as time went by.

Something was wrong.

I shoved my hand into my bra and pulled out the phone and dialed his number, panicking.

He answered after a few rings.

"Vincent?"

"Myra? What's wrong? Why are you talking like that?" He asked, sounding more concerned after each question.

"Please. Help me. I don't what's happening." I mumbled.

"Where are you, baby?"

I tried to answer, and tried to fight the sudden fatigue. I heard shuffling over the phone.

"Myra?" He said again.

"Ben... brought me somewhere. Please..."

"I'm coming. Stay where you are!"

The phone slipped from my hand as I lost control of my body.

I heard a sudden pounding against the door, but couldn't find the energy to open it.

The last thing I saw was Ben rushing in and grabbing me before I fell on the floor.

Then everything darkened.

◻°•◻◻_____◻◻•°◻

So here is the next chapter. Its currently 4am. I've been trying to write it for so long, but kept getting distracted.

Also sorry if there are mistakes. I got my nails done and typing with them is really hard lmao.

Let me know what you think.

Please don't forget to Vote, Comment and Share.

Z.A.B

chapter 26

▫ Warning : contains drug use, rape, extreme violence. Please do not read if triggered. ▫°•▫▫_____▫▫•°▫

He glared at the ceiling, laying in bed with an arm behind his head. He hated being away from her. Part of him wished that he refused Ben's new deal and stuck with the six months he had given to him. At least by the end of it, Ben would have been out of the picture. He would've had Myra all to himself. He could touch her whenever he wanted, see her, just sleep with her.

He couldn't control his anger, whilst talking to her and he knew his outburst had hurt her. She was sensitive and sweet, something he had learned within the first few days of living with her. But he still hated how much control she had over him. He regretted pursuing her this way, he should've waited until six months were over before going anywhere near her, but he couldn't help himself.

Everything about her called to him. He'd never even met with anyone like her, it made him think that perhaps... she was the one for him. Even when in the beginning she was afraid of even looking at him, now she had the guts to speak up against him. She stood up to him. She trusted him. He gulped at the realisation.

He felt guilty about the way he made her leave, he knew he would cave before she even said a word to him. It was his fault that they were both in this situation.

He took a deep breath to relax and closed his eyes, falling asleep quickly.

☐°•☐☐_____☐☐•°☐

A loud ring awoke him from his sleep. He reached for his phone with annoyance, answering it without checking the caller ID.

"Vincent."

His heart dropped to his stomach. His name slightly sounded slurred.

"Myra? What's wrong? Why are you talking like that?" He asked, sounding more concerned after each question.

"Please. Help me. I don't know what's happening." She mumbled.

"Where are you, baby?" He asked desperately, already out of bed and dressing himself up.

There was silence for a moment, he could hear her moaning a little in an attempt to answer.

"Myra?" He said again.

"Ben... brought me somewhere. Please..."

"I'm coming. Stay where you are!" He heard the phone drop and then some shuffling.

He ran down towards Sam's room, kicking the door open. The room was filled with groans and moans which were cut off as soon as Sam heard the door slam open into the wall.

"What the fuck, Vincent?" Growled Sam, climbing off his girlfriend.

"Just because you're not getting some, doesn't mean no one else can either."

Once Sam looked at his face he realised something was not right.

"It's Myra."

That was all he needed to hear before leaving his girl in bed, confused.

"I'll make it up to you, baby." He promised, pulling his pants on and grabbing his weapons. Vincent was already on the phone calling back up and then checked her phone location. He didn't need to call a specialist to find her location. He opened the tracking app and tapped her location, sharing it with the few members of his back up team. He knew it was wrong to spy on her, but it was the only thing keeping him sane. He thanked whatever being that was above him that she took the phone with herself regardless of what he said in the heat of the moment.

They left in a hurry with Vincent in the passenger seat and Sam driving to the location was thirty minutes away, but they had to hurry. He could feel something very had was going to happen.

And he was ready to go to any extent to save her.

☐°•☐☐_____☐☐•°☐

Everything was blurry, it sounded as if people were speaking from a distance and their voices echoed. Her whole body was lacking control. She managed to force her eyes open and found herself in an unfamiliar room.

It was difficult for her to remember how she even got here. She tried to blink quickly to clear her sight, but it was all in slow motion.

Myra turned her head to see Ben sitting on a sofa opposite another man. Frederick.

Her body felt hot and she was sweating, but she wasn't able to tell. She lost touch with reality.

"Is she a virgin?" Asked Frederick, eyeing her body. Her dress had ridden up to her thighs.

"Yes. Most definitely. You know how their people are, they are old fashioned. They consider the purity of a woman as the highest regard." Answered Ben, rolling his eyes.

"Oh, but it is. There something addicting about virgins. The innocence. The fear. It is an ever lasting imprint you leave on a woman. Their pain, is the greatest pleasure a man can receive." He grinned sickly.

"How so?" Asked Ben.

"It is the tightest they will ever be. It's a shame that she will probably not remember it in the morning. Your money is in the briefcase. You can stay here and watch or find that bitch and enjoy yourself." He stated, referring to his fake fiancé.

Ben stayed and watched his friend climb on the bed, between her legs. He held her knees and spread her even further.

Myra moaned as she felt his hand on her. Her eyes were closed again.

He tugged the dress down her body, exposing her bra cladded breasts. His mouth watered at the sight, she truly was a prize.

"Your husband is fucking blind." He muttered, tracing his finger tips over her plump lips.

There was nothing she could do to protest.

"The best part is, I'll fuck you raw and I have all night to impregnate you."

Myra opened her mouth to say something, but the words were just not coming out, instead moaned in protest.

"You like that? You dirty little slut." He growled lowly. He pushed her dress higher, baring her lower half. He rubbed his fingers over her sex, groaning at the slight wetness.

"You don't even need foreplay. You'll be so sore tomorrow, but will have no idea why." He continued to whisper. Myra tried to shake her head. She couldn't understand why her body was so warm and aroused.

He had vile grin on his lecherous face. He gripped the edge of her underwear pulling them off and bringing them to his nose and groaned. He couldn't waste those. He shoved them into his pocket, keeping them as a souvenir.

"Open your eyes, bitch!" He ordered loudly. He grabbed her face between his fingers, squeezing painfully hard. She whimpered, forcing her eyes open. She looked towards him, her eyes filling with tears and then her husband. She couldn't react fast enough.

The so called fiancé had joined him, her head bobbing up and down on his lap. She hoped Ben would look at her; have som sort of mercy, but when he did, his expression was hard.

"I want her next."

Myra panicked, she felt like she couldn't breathe anymore. More tears fell from her eyes and she looked back at Frederick who began unbuttoning his pants, and pulling down the zipper.

She couldn't fight, her limbs felt too heavy to move. She gave up. This was her fate. Her own husband was going to rape her.

He pressed erect penis against her wet slit, gliding it up and down, before aligning himself. He pressed against her with the slightest pressure then pulling away, teasing himself.

A loud crash caused the three of them to jump. The door slammed open, revealing Vincent and his men.

He took in the sight of Myra laying on the bed defenselessly with her eyes closed. His heart dropped.

His face turned deadly as he looked at the man between her legs. His rage blinded him, but the psychotic part of him didn't react.

"Come here." He ordered Frederick, who had paled at the sight of the powerful man.

He stood up from the bed, cautiously moved towards him. Without another thought Vincent raised his gun and pulled the trigger, aimed towards his crotch.

A piercing scream left his mouth as he clutched his crotch in his hand and fell on the floor. Blood spurted all over the floor, colouring the expensive carpet.

Vincent smiled at the sight. He cracked his neck, before turning to look at her husband, who sat there shocked and restrained by Sam.

"Is this how you were planning to repay me?" He asked calmly, settling down on the cushioned luxury chairs. Ben struggled to answer out of pure fear.

"I had no choice." He whimpered pathetically.

Vincent threw his head back and laughed, before glaring at him fiercely.

"So you sell your wife? You're a pathetic excuse for a man. This agreement is over and you will pay me with your life."

"Why do you care?" He screamed in panic, delaying his death.

"She is mine." He answered simply.

Vincent stood up, standing in front of Ben, cooking his gun. He pressed the cold gun under his chin, resting his finger on the trigger.

"Take her, spare me." He begged, pleading for his life. Tears fell down his face.

Vincent clenched his jaw tightly in anger.

"Too late."

Before Ben could react, Vincent pressed down on the trigger a loud bang echoed the room once again. This time blood and brains splattered over the walls. Sam released Ben's lifeless body, causing it to drop to the ground.

He turned to look at Frederick who was still alive and heard every part of the exchange between them.

"I didn't know!" He pleaded shaking his head at Vincent who cooked his gun, shooting him in the shoulder.

"Sam. Try to miss the vitals, make it last as long as possible." He said over his shoulder as he moved closer to her.

"With pleasure, boss." He answered cheerily.

Vincent felt everything block out into the background, the cries and screams of pain and the continuous gun shots.

He placed his hand on her cheek, her skin burning him. She shifted and opened her eyes fearfully.

Vincent watched her eyes staring up at him, recognition glittering in them. Her eyes filled with tears and spilled over her cheeks like a waterfall.

"V... Vi-" She slurred sleepily.

"Shhhh, Myra. Go to sleep." He mumbled, wiping her tears, feeling his own burning.

Her forehead creased and he saw fear in them.

"Do you trust me? If you do then close your eyes. I'll take care of you. I promise, with my life."

She was taking shaky breaths, trying to relax. With one more pleading look, she closed her eyes. Then there was silence. It was over.

He turned around, noticing a blonde head hiding away behind the bigger sofa. He called in a member of his back up and dragged her out.

Never leave any witnessed behind, that was his motto.

"We've got to get her to the hospital. Hurry up." Ordered Sam. There was no time for regrets now. Vincent nodded mutely and lifted her into his arms, holding her against himself tightly and carried her to the car as Sam ordered the rest of the team to clean up and leave everything spotless.

He sat in the back clutching her tightly, hoping that she was fine and partially wishing that she does not remember anything.

▫°•▫▫_____▫▫•°▫

Omg. That was quite long isn't it.

Completed at 5am. I'm gonna love reading the comments when I wake up

I'm not really sure how the drug stuff works, but it's as accurate as I imagine it to be through research. Please let me know how you found it.

How are we all feeling. I think that was the most intense violent scene I have ever imagined and written. I hope it was good enough.

Please remember to Vote, Comment and Share.

Z.A.B

chapter 27

The smell of disinfectant lingered in the air as the steady beep of the monitor filled the silence. It had been a some time since they had arrived at the private hospital. He couldn't take her anywhere, without having to get the authorities involved.

Vincent held her hand as he slept on the chair beside her bed whilst leaning his head on his folded arms. He had been staying with her as much as he could. The doctors had to force him out of the room for their examination. They had been informed of the situation and wanted to make sure that there was nothing to worry about.

The doctors also informed him that she should regain consciousness within the next day, depending on how quickly her body could get rid of the drug.

Her hand twitched a little causing him to jerk awake. He blinked a couple of times before focusing on her face to see any signs of her waking up, but it seemed that she was still asleep.

Myra whimpered in her unconscious state, feeling drowsy and heavy, but forced herself to wake up.

He punched the button on the side alerting the doctors to visit her room as soon as possible. The doctor entered her room very quickly and checked her eyes and breathing.

"It seems she's gaining consciousness." He stated, nervously when Vincent glared at him.

Myra opened her eyes, frowning when the bright light hurt her eyes. His glare quickly changed into concern when she blinked to clear her vision.

She looked around the white room with confusion. Something was not right. She couldn't remember a thing. Her heart raced and she began panicking, with the monitor picking up on everything.

She looked to her side, where she saw him sitting beside her bed. He could see that she was trying to understand what had happened.

"I understand you are confused, Ms Myra. Please do not panic. I regret to inform you, that you were drugged."

Her eyes widened shock, she remembered that she went out with Ben quite clearly.

"You may still feel some symptoms. The drug should flush out within 12 hours. So we will keep you here."

She opened her mouth to speak, but her throat felt too dry. She coughed, putting her hand over her mouth.

Vincent immediately grabbed a bottle of water and opened it, raising it to her lips. She looked up at him and he could see the questions in her eyes. She drank from the bottle eagerly, not realising that she was so thirsty.

"I would recommend you drink as much water as possible, it will remove the toxins from your body quicker." Said the doctor, glancing at Vincent again.

"I have received your other reports as well." He stated.

He waited for Myra to finish drinking before turning his attention to the doctor again.

"I understand he mentioned that he found you under unfortunate circumstances. Your tests show there were no signs of forced penetration vaginally or anally. The nurse also took swabs of her vagina, but the tests showed nothing. You have nothing to worry about. The blood report showed you had a typical date rape drug used, as I mentioned before that you will be perfectly fine in a few hours. I'll have to get going, if you need anything else please let me know." He said pursing his lips.

"Thank you, doctor."

Shock covered the doctors face for a moment before he nodded and left.

She stared at Vincent the whole time as he explained his report.

"What- what happened?" She whispered, afraid to hear the truth.

"Frederick drugged you." He answered.

"B-but Ben was there."

"Myra... he was selling you for sex."

She swallowed her emotions for the moment.

"Where are they now?"

"Dead."

She wanted to allow herself to hyperventilate, but didn't. She stayed quiet. Vincent held her hand again, but she pulled it out of his grip, turning the other, closing her eyes.

She didn't see the hurt that crossed his face at her action. He stayed quiet, settling down in the chair beside her again. He leaned back and closed his eyes again, trying to sleep.

They rested for a little while longer again, until she woke up again needing to use the toilet. She climbed out carefully keeping most of her weight on against the bed.

She gasped as she stumbled causing Vincent to jerk away again. He couldn't relax until he was sure she was safe.

He stood up abruptly rushing to her and holding her up.

"What is it?" He asked gently.

She pushed his hands away, but he didn't relent and instead tightened his hold on her. "Need to pee."

He picked her up in his arms without any strain and carried her to the joined bathroom, placing her right beside the toilet.

"Call me when you're done."

She didn't say anything and watched him leave. Vincent leaned against the wall right outside, waiting to hear from her. It was only a few minutes before she opened the door, causing him to give her another disapproving glare. She ignored him and sat down on the bed again.

Just then the doctor walked in again, holding a clipboard.

"It's safe to discharge you now, Ms Myra. Unless you have any other concerns." The doctor suggested. Myra shook her head, staring at the floor.

The doctor passed Vincent the clipboard and he signed it. He walked to Myra, handing her a bag of clothes to wear. He wanted to know what she was thinking, desperately.

"I'll wait outside." He muttered.

He texted Sam that they were leaving and informed the driver to be ready.

After some times, she finally emerged from the room, wearing a black dress which came up to her knees. Her hair was put in a loose bun and they walked to the car. She walked a few steps behind him, crossing her arms.

Vincent carefully sat Myra into his car, closing the door. He was worried about her.

He expected her to wake up and cry, but she stayed silent, calm, too calm to be normal. He was expecting something similar to her reaction when he pulled a gun on her, but there was nothing. Her expression remained stoic, there was no sadness, no hurt, nothing.

He sat down next to her, signalling his driver to start driving back to his home. The silence was killing him. Myra's hands were shaking as she sat beside him. He gently grasped her hand in his larger one, reminding her silently that she was safe and nothing would happen to her again.

She gave him no response, nothing to say that she noticed him, instead just stared out of the tinted windows.

He leaned back against his seat, staring ahead. They were now halfway back to his home.

"I want to go home... to see my parents." She stated looking up at him. He stared at her blankly. She hadn't spoken about her parents again since the last time she mentioned them.

Hesitantly, he nodded. She told him where they lived, which was a 2 hour drive from his home. He noticed her relief at his answer and calmed a little.

She shuffled closer to him, leaning her head on his shoulder. He lifted hand, cupping her face gently and stroking her cheek before dropping it in his lap, keeping hold of her hand.

He sighed, at last she said something. Myra closed her eyes, deciding to sleep and prepare for the emotional confrontation she was going to have with her parents.

After a long drive, the driver stopped. Vincent gently woke Myra up from her nap, careful not to startle her. She sat up abruptly looking around confused. "Myra, were here." He said softly. She looked out the window, gulping before opening the passenger door, stepping out with Vincent right behind her.

She straightened her dress out and cleared her throat staring at the small house. She took small steps to the front door. She took a deep breath and raised her hand and knocked on the door.

There was silence. Her shoulders slumped with defeat and she turned around, looking at the floor. Vincent walked towards her and wrapped his arms around her.

"I'm sorry."

▢°•▢▢_____▢▢•°▢

I'm in such a good mood nowadays and it really helps me write.

How would you feel about a double update since I'm feeling so generous

I know it's not a long chapter, but what do you think?

I feel bad for putting her through so much crap.

Leave your thoughts, likes and share!!!

Z.A.B

chapter 28

Just as they began walking away, she heard the door open.

She quickly turned around, looking to see her mother peeking out from the door. "M-Myra?" She stammered, shocked. "Mum!" She cried. Her mother pushed the rest of the door open quickly pulling Myra into a tight embrace.

"I missed you so much." She sobbed loudly, sounding choked up.

"What-" said another voice from her house. "Myra?" He said before pulling his daughter into a hug. Vincent watched the whole scene play out quietly. They all cried together for a few minutes, before her Father pulled away, wiping her tears and kissing her forehead.

"What are you doing here? Did Ben allow you to come and see us? Who's the man behind you?" He bombarded. Vincent narrowed his eyes, understanding why she was so nervous about meeting her parents. Ben probably didn't allow her to see them.

"Dad, so much happened. I don't even know where to start." She cried.

"Let's go inside. We can talk all about it." Suggested her mother.

She nodded and turned around, gesturing for him to come in by holding her hand out. He hesitated, but she gave him a small smile inviting him in. His heart warmed up at her smile. Her cheeks were wet and eyes still watery.

They sat down on the sofa, Vincent sitting beside her and her parents opposite them.

"Where is Ben?" Asked her Father again, more concerned than before. He could tell Myra was not well. She had lost too much weight since her wedding day. The glimmer of happiness in her eyes had dimmed down a lot.

"He is dead." She stated with tears in her eyes.

Both her parents gasped at the sudden demise of her husband.

"What happened?" Asked her Mother.

"Vincent... Vincent killed him." She whispered.

Her Father stood up enraged, grabbing him by the collar and dragging him up. Myra's eyes widened, she'd never seen her Father so angry before to raise a hand on someone else.

"You son of a -"

"Dad, let go of him." She screamed, pushing her Father off him, standing in front of him protectively.

Her Father froze.

"If it wasn't for him, I wouldn't be here today." She said quietly. Vincent sat her back down, keeping his hand on her waist. Her Father glared at him.

"Ben lied about everything. His wealth, his job and his property. He didn't own anything. That money he had... it belonged to Vincent. It was a loan. And it was time to pay it back.

Ben gave me to him to use as he intended, in an exchange for more time. This all happened within a month of my marriage. I stayed with Vincent for three months. Ben paid him half and promised to pay the rest once he had me back.

I went back and everything seemed normal, but then we went out on a date, because he wanted to make things better between us. We went to his friends house... and he drugged me. He was going to sell me to get the rest of the money. If Vincent hadn't arrived in time... I don't even know if I would've been alive."

Her parents stayed silent with shock of everything that had happened to their daughter in the past few months.

It had taken her a few hours to explain everything, answering more questions that her parents had about her marriage, with breaks in between as Vincent rubbed his hand over her back soothingly. He took out a napkin and gave it to her, she dabbed her eyes gently; wiping away the remaining tears. Once she was done, she was exhausted.

"Excuse me." He said standing up and walking to the front to door and standing outside. He wanted to give them some time alone to comfort their daughter.

He wasn't sure how long he waited outside, but it was getting dark now. "Vincent?" She called out sweetly. He turned around to look at her.

"Can I... stay the night?" She asked pleadingly, begging him with her brown eyes. "I- I promise I won't to ask you for anything else. I won't see them again, please." She added quickly.

"I'll come to pick you up tomorrow." He stated, walking towards his car. She quickly halted him, grabbing his hand. "Don't leave." She whispered.

"I'm not wanted here, Myra." He said without turning to look at her.

"I want you here. Please?" She said quietly. He slowly turned to look at her and could not refuse her pouting cutely at him. He sighed, before agreeing with a nod of his head.

They both walked back inside the house this time, there were two younger girls sitting in the room, which he assumed were her younger siblings.

"Vincent, meet my younger sisters, Syra and Nyma." She introduced proudly. Both sisters waved back with a small smile. Both sisters had short black hair, completely straight, a contrast from Myra's long brown curly hair.

"Hi, it's nice to meet you both." He said lifting his hand to shake. They both looked at each other hesitantly then peeked up at Myra, who nodded at them. "I don't bite. Ask your sister." He half smiled. Myra cleared her throat knowing that was a lie and hid her smile.

Myra already felt better being around her family, almost forgetting what happened. She didn't want to think about it while she was here, so she kept it at the back of her mind. "Girls, come and prepare for Dinner." Shouted their Mother from the Kitchen.

She squeezed his hand lightly, leaving him in the room with her Father, in an awkward silence. After a few moments, he cleared his throat walking up to Vincent. "Thank you for saving my daughter... and I'm sorry for my previous actions." He said stiffly, holding his hand out.

Vincent glanced at him, he was the same height as him. "There's nothing to thank me for and nothing to apologise for." He answered, shaking his hand. He nodded in response. "Come sit." He said walking towards their Dinner table.

While the men sat down and started their awkward small talk, Myra was actively helping her Mother preparing the food. "Did you make anything less spicy?" She asked, pulling out the plates. "Why?" Asked her Mother.

"Vincent doesn't like spicy food." She stated with a blush. Her Mother paused what she was doing, looking up at her daughter. "Myra, is there something I should know?" She asked.

"I-I don't know what you're talking about." She stuttered. "Young lady, I know you haven't seen me for a few months, but I'm still your Mother." She scolded.

"I like him." She muttered, crossing her arms. "You know he's dangerous." She said gently, but her daughter frowned at her.

"He's still better than Ben. He respects me and took care of me." She argued.

"Does he like you too?" She asked, making Myra pause. She didn't know the answer to that question. "Yes, but even if he doesn't, I owe him my life." She answered embarrassed.

"I'm sure he does, sweetheart. I could see the way he looked at you whilst you were crying." She smiled. Myra blushed, looking down.

"I made rice and chicken, just give him some yoghurt on the side." She said answering her earlier question.

Myra took the steaming pot of rice inside, placing it on the table, before sitting beside Vincent, giving him a small smile.

She waited for her Mother to serve everyone before grabbing a plate for Vincent and putting a little bit of Chicken and Rice in it with some yoghurt. He nodded at her. "Mix it together, it might be too spicy." She said giving him a rueful smile. Both of their minds reeled back to the first time they cooked together, making him smile. Both of them were unaware that the whole table was watching them, everyone smiling except her Father.

▫°•▫▫_____▫▫•°▫

Here is your double update. I hope its okay.

I think after all that she deserved seeing her family. Let's see what they have to say about him.

Please don't forget to comment, Vote and Share.

Z.A.B

chapter 29

Dinner went better than she had imagined, she was sure her Father was going to have a word with her about Vincent. She wasn't sure what she would say, but she wasn't going to leave him no matter what.

Her parents cleaned up after Dinner leaving the rest of them at the table. Myra moved everyone to the sofas where they sat together, having their usual banter.

"Is that gun real?" Asked Syra, she was the youngest, only 16 years old. Vincent nodded, glancing at Myra. "Can I hold it?" She asked shyly.

"No!" Interjected Myra, it wasn't a toy to pass to children. "Please Myra. I just want to see it." She pouted.

Vincent pulled the gun out of his holster, unloading it and passing it to her sister. "Vincent! I said no." She said narrowing her eyes angrily. "I've taken the magazine out. It's fine." He said rolling his eyes.

"You're going to be such a terrible Father." She said crossing her arms. "Not with you around." He answered. Myra was taken aback by his answer, her lips parted with surprise, but she said nothing else.

Nyma coughed, diverting their attention back to the rest of them. "Syra, give it back before Dad sees it on you." She scolded. Syra pouted again holding the gun out to Vincent who took it from her and secured it back into the holster.

"Come on everyone, it's bedtime." Said her Mother, walking in. "Mum, is it okay if I sleep in your room?" She asked looking at the floor.

"Of course sweetheart." She smiled. Myra had a lot of things to say. "Why don't you put Vincent in your room and come when you're done."

Myra nodded, standing up and looking down at Vincent who didn't get up yet. "Are you coming?" She asked raising her brow. He smirked getting up. He was going to be sleeping in her room, which meant he was free to explore it.

He followed her through the house where they stopped outside her room. She slowly opened the door, turning on the lights. She stood there for a moment, looking at her small bed on the side of the room where she spent a long time studying and doing homework. Then her a small cupboard where she kept a few books that she owned. It was pretty much empty and small. Myra stepped in walking over to the small picture frame of herself and her sisters.

"Myra." He called gently. She turned around and looked up at him. "Are you alright?" He asked concerned. Her behaviour was unusual, sure she had cried but he expected more emotions. "Yes. I'm just trying not to think about it. I feel safer with my family. And with you."

He walked up to her, wrapping his arm around her waist. "I'm sorry I sent you back. I should've known he was going to do something stupid." He apologised, kissing her forehead. "How could you have known?" She asked, placing her hands on his chest, playing with the button of his shirt. "I just should've." He whispered, leaning down to her.

"I'm sorry for ignoring you."

"Myra, you don't have to apologise. You've just gone through something traumatising." He frowned, rubbing her back. She pulled him into a tight embrace, wrapping her arms around him. Myra felt her emotions bubbling up again, pressing her face into his chest. He held her while she cried softly, sniffling.

After a few minutes, she pulled away. "You look beautiful even when you cry." He said, wiping her tears. She let out a partial sob and giggle, shaking her head. "I'm going to grab my clothes."

She opened her cupboard, looking at her old clothes. Myra loved dressing casual, jeans and t-shirts were her go-to clothes, but Ben never allowed her to wear them. He preferred dresses, mostly formal ones. She pulled out her favourite black superman shirt and black sweatpants, before turning to look at him, clutching her clothes to her chest.

She looked up at him gulping at the heated look on his face. "Goodnight." She whispered, walking over to the door. "Myra." She froze, turning around and looking up at him.

He walked over to her, backing her up against the door. "Can I kiss you?" He asked leaning down, pressing his forehead against hers. She blushed, biting her lip before answering. "You don't have to ask." She said in a quiet voice. He didn't waste another second, pressing his lips to her soft ones, groaning. It felt like an eternity had passed since he last kissed her.

She dropped her clothes, wrapping her arms around his neck and pulling him down. He bent down lifting her so she wrapped her legs around him. "Don't drop me." She panicked against his mouth. He chuckled, biting her lip. "I'm stronger than you think." He answered.

He slid his tongue into her mouth, coaxing hers forwards too. He sucked on it, tangling it with his. She moaned against his mouth.

She pulled away blushing. "What happened?" He asked, kissing her cheek. "Someone might hear." She panted. "So?" He asked narrowing his eyes at her.

She gulped again. "I- I need to clear some things up with my parents... about us."

"What are you going to say?" He asked, pulling her ass up higher.

"I don't know." She mumbled, fiddling with the collar of his shirt.

"Tell them you're mine." He growled possessively. She gasped, her eyes snapping up to his.

"Are you mine too?" She asked quietly, immediately regretting it. He owned her, whether she wanted him or not.

She kept her eyes locked with his, wanting to know the truth, but Vincent knew they hadn't established their relationship. "Yes."

Her blush came back full force, her face breaking out in a big smile. He slowly let her down, bending down to grab her clothes and holding them out to her.

She leaned up giving him a short peck, before opening the door. "Goodnight."

He smiled at her. Her heart fluttered, it was still unusual to see him smiling so openly, it made him look so carefree, handsome.

She walked out and he watched her until she disappeared down the hall readying herself to confront her Father.

☐°•☐☐_____☐☐•°☐

She stepped into their bedroom after knocking, unsure of where to start the conversation. Her Father sat on the bed already in his pyjamas as he waited for her to speak.

"Are you going back with him?" He asked, starting the conversation.

"Yes, Father." She nodded, fidgeting with her fingers.

"Why?"

"I owe him."

"And what else?"

"I- I like him." She whispered, her heart pounding.

"So you're willing to stay with him, even if decides to make you his mistress?" He asked angrily.

"He- he wouldn't do that." She mumbled shaking her head.

"How would you know?"

"Because he's never done anything against my will."

"And you know what the future holds?" He scoffed.

"Did you know what the future holds when you decided to marry me off to Ben?" She asked, looking up at her father with disbelief.

He clenched his jaw angrily.

"You're saying it like I forced you." He argued.

"No, you did not. But you did your best to persuade me. You knew it wasn't difficult to convince me. I did that for you. And now that I want to decide for myself, it is wrong? All of a sudden I should be more concerned about what Vincent is like? For your information, Father, I have spent more time with him rather than my actual husband. He didn't bully me into changing myself, or treat me like a I was his carer instead of a wife." She vented, her father was taken aback by her outburst.

"You're not going with him." He said raising his voice slightly.

"I am going with him, whether you like it or not." She stated firmly.

"Just because you are older, does not mean you are right. After everything that everyone's decisions have put me through, I will not listen."

He stood up and laid down on his side of the bed, furious at her. She had never argued with him over anything.

Myra turned her teary eyes to her Mother, who was already coming over to consolidate her. They walked out of the room, back into the living room and sat down.

"Don't worry about him, Myra." She soothed, rubbing her back.

"Why is he so unfair? I've always done everything you guys have asked me for. I never refused anything that you said. I married Ben for everyone's sake. Am I not allowed to be happy? Am I not allowed to be in charge of my own life? Even if it's temporary, I want it. I just want to be happy, is that too much to ask for?" She questioned, sobbing loudly.

"Shhh. Ignore him. He is just angry at himself. He feels as though everything is his fault. You have gone through things that he had never even dreamed of. He is just feeling overprotective. Trust me everything will be fine in the morning." Her Mother assured. She knew her husband was a stubborn man, but she knew how to get through him too. It's what she had learned after to many years of marriage.

"Where do you want to sleep?" Asked her Mother.

"Here is fine." She mumbled, wiping her tears away.

"Okay, let me grab you a blanket and pillow."

After her Mother brought all her things to her, she laid down on the sofa. She desperately wanted to see Vincent, but she knew if she went in he wouldn't let her out until the morning. Part of her wasn't able to believe that he was down the hall from her. So close.

She closed her eyes, falling asleep fairly quickly after the emotional roller coasters she had to go through.

□°•□□_____□□•°□

Myra woke up earlier than everyone, just like she was accustomed to. She forced her sisters out of bed out of pure boredom. After much complaining, they got up and sat together in the living room.

They were all laughing and joking around until Vincent decided to join them. Vincent stared at Myra, dressed so casually, laughing freely with her siblings. She had a glow on her face despite what she had gone through. He enjoyed seeing her carefree attitude. She was laying down on the sofa, with her hair sprawled out over the edge as she mentioned something embarrassing she did when she was younger.

He walked in and Myra's laugh dried in her throat. Vincent was shirtless. She stared at his bare chest, blushing fiercely before looking away from him.

She quickly sat up, straightening her back. It all seemed formal now. He came and sat down right beside her. "Go put your clothes on." She muttered leaning further away from him. "Why? Are you getting distracted?" He smirked leaning closer to her. She shook her head shyly, peeking up at her sisters who were also watching him with their mouths dropped open.

She narrowed her eyes at her siblings and was just about to tell them off, but stopped. What was that feeling?

Jealousy?

Myra hardly got jealous, but they were openly gawking at him and obviously he noticed. "Syra, Nyma, why don't you start preparing breakfast and I'll come and help you." She suggested and watched as they both snapped out of their daze, blushing with embarrassment.

She watched them leave, before looking up at him. He gave her a knowing smile. "I like seeing you like this." He said gently, putting his arm around her shoulder. She gave him a confused look. "So carefree. Casual. Then when I came in you sat up straighter than a ruler." She smacked his thigh, defensively.

"I'm just used to being like that around others." She mumbled self-consciously.

"Oh. So I'm just 'others' to you." He nodded, pulling away from her.

"That's not what I meant!" She panicked. "I just thought you liked seeing me... I mean, men like seeing women all proper and dressed up."

"You don't need to dress to impress me. And as much as I love those short sexy dresses you wear, I prefer seeing you as you feel comfortable. You dress up for yourself, not for someone else."

She blushed looking down at her lap. He pulled her into his lap holding her against himself. "Vincent... someone will see." She muttered pulling away from him.

"I don't care." He stated, kissing her lips. He pushed his hand under her shirt. Myra melted into his touch, placing her hands on his shoulders. She shuddered feeling his strong muscles flexing as he cupped her breast in one hand.

She pulled away from his mouth, kissing down his jaw to his neck. She'd been daring before, but she never left a mark on him. She bit his skin, moaning as he squeezed her breast. She sucked his skin into her mouth a little harder than he did. He groaned lowly. She pulled away looking at him. "Did it hurt?"

"No, don't stop." He whispered pulling her back down. He watched as her face warmed up. She leaned forwards again, biting his neck playfully. He grunted, squeezing her hips.

She laughed and pulled away again. "Somebody is feeling naughty." He smirked. He grabbed the back of her head pulling her down, biting her lip. She gasped, Vincent took the chance of slipping his tongue into her mouth.

"Myra- oh-"

She jumped off his lap, looking up to see Nyma standing in the doorway with her hands over her eyes.

She peeked up at Vincent to see him smirking at her. She quickly got off the sofa and walked to the kitchen without a word.

▫°•▫▫_____▫▫•°▫

So another update lol.

So I just wanted to let you guys know that we are slowly reaching the end of this book. I'm sure some people think it is too short, but I didn't think it would be more than 20 chapters. There is nothing more i can add to it and i dont want to make it drag. I would say about 4 more chappies and then it will end.

I wrote the hospital after chapter 6, way before anything else I had written.

Anyways as usual, please leave your comments, votes and share!

Z.A.B

chapter 30

"Myra, we're leaving tonight." He informed me carefully. I felt myself becoming emotional again, so I nodded in response.

"Come here, baby." He murmured.

"I know I'm not allowed to come here and I have accepted that. I won't-"

He tugged me towards himself, placing his hands on my waist.

"Am I like Ben?" He questioned, raising an eyebrow.

I shook my head, looking away.

"Then why do you think I would forbid you from seeing your family?"

"I just... don't want to be a burden."

He made a disapproving tut and I bit my lip harshly.

"You're not my hostage anymore. You're free to do what you like, stay where you like. Just let me know." He stated softly.

I wrapped my arms around him tightly, maybe it was finally my time to be happy. A man that was feared by a lot of people was standing in front of me, allowing me to do as I pleased.

"Thank you." I mumbled.

"'Thank you' won't be enough." He teased. I pulled away, a smile graced my lips. "What will I have to do?" I asked innocently, tilting my head to the side.

"You will have to wait until we get home to find out, baby-girl." He smirked. I felt my face warming up with all the different things that went through my mind.

My mind stopped on one thing I knew I wasn't ready for. Sex. He had never pressured me, but I knew it was kind of expected. I just couldn't after everything, even though I don't really remember it. It's all just a haze in my mind. I do remember hearing a lot of gunshots, but wondered if it was my imagination or side effects of the drug.

I felt much better. I knew the symptoms were now gone.

"What's wrong, Myra?" He asked, all signs of playfulness leaving his face.

I shook my head quickly, stepping away from him.

He didn't question me, but continued to stare at me. "Shall we sit with the rest?" I asked, hoping he would agree without anymore questions.

He nodded. I sighed with relief and then held my hand out to him. He smiled a little, enveloping it in his bigger one as I led him to the living room. We stepped in and everyone's eyes turned to us, then to our joined hands. I looked at my Father and he glared at our hands. He had to accept it. He didn't have another choice.

Both my sisters stood from the sofa and made space for us to sit down. I couldn't guarantee anything from my Father, but my siblings made sure he didn't feel left out. They were so sweet. I know they wanted someone to bond with, but Ben forced me to cut my family off.

"What are you planning to do, Syra?" He asked, on a serious note.

"I -I want to be a teacher." She answered nervously. She was a little more shy than all of us. "That's great. Have you looked into paths?"

She shook her head timidly. "Not yet, Sir"

"What about you, Nyma?" He said turning his attention to my other sibling.

"Something to do with computing? Maybe computer science, but it really depends on..." she stopped, glancing at me hesitantly.

"On what?" He pressed on.

"Finance." She mumbled.

He nodded understandingly.

She quickly changed the topic. "Do you know what Myra wanted to be?"

He shook his head. "Nothing!" I interjected quickly.

"A writer."

"Oh, really?" He asked sounding genuinely surprised.

"It's nothing. I'd probably be really bad at it and it doesn't really require much academic achievement, which means it's not enough to support anyone." Shurgging it off with embarrassment.

"There's nothing wrong with trying it out." He stated.

"Myra had the best grades in her class. She can do anything she wants once she puts her mind to it." Added Nyma.

He hummed in response, watching me. I cleared my throat awkwardly.

Thankfully, the topic changed quickly and I relaxed into the sofa. He probably thought I was so lame compared to my siblings. I picked a different career path because I knew there's not much hope for new authors.

"I'm going to start on Dinner, okay?" Said her Mother getting up. My dad joined her, completely ignoring me.

"Are you okay?" He asked softly. I felt a lump forming in my throat and I shook my head. Thankfully, he didn't press it on any further. I didn't want to cry again, not yet anyways.

I leaned my head on his shoulder, wrapping my arms around his muscly one and holding it tightly.

My sisters chattered away with Vincent for a long time. They liked him and that made me happier than anything in the world. I knew Vincent would take care of them too.

Dinner was quieter between myself and my parents, but my sisters continued to joke around with him while they ate. When it was over, I avoided looking at Vincent knowing that he would gesture than it is time to leave.

I dreaded the moment we were alone because he would talk to me.

"Myra..."

I nodded without looking at him and put on my flats and a coat of mine.

Everyone came into the living room again and were quiet, except my Father who was no where to be seen. My lip began trembling and tears burned my eyes. I took deep breaths to calm myself, but I knew it was inevitable.

My mother came forwards and I took a step back. "Don't."

"Oh Myra." She sighed softly. "It's okay. Your don't have to be strong now of all time."

I hugged her tightly and sobbed, trying to keep it down. My sisters were also crying a little bit. I held her for some time before I felt myself calming down a little more.

I hugged both my sisters and they held my hand tightly.

When all the goodbyes were done I turned to look at him who was watching me, somewhat sad that I was crying.

"Myra." I froze.

I turned around to see my Father standing there slightly teary eyed. I ran to him and hugged him as tightly as I could.

"Take care of yourself. If you think this is your way to happiness, then I accept it. I don't want you to leave thinking I'm angry at you. You're old enough to make your own decisions."

I felt so much relief flooding through me at the words that came out of his mouth, that I felt myself smiling.

"Thank you, Dad." I mumbled into his shirt. I stood sideways and saw both my sisters running up to Vincent and grabbing a hand each, tugging it to catch his attention.

"Will Myra be allowed to visit?" They asked in unison, looking up at him with wide eyes.

"Of course. You're all most welcome to come and visit too." He nodded and they both hugged him. He looked down a little surprised and back up at me. I smiled even more seeing they have bonded with him. He patted their heads and smiled a little.

"Here you go. You can call me to arrange anything." He gave them both a business card with his personal number on it. He urged the two siblings out with himself.

My Father watched them leave with him and looked down at me. I could see the sadness in his eyes, but I guess we both knew that I was allowed to visit without any conditions. It didn't make it that bad.

"Call me when you can." He smiled softly. I nodded and we all stepped out of the house.

I left his side and stood next to Vincent, linking my fingers with his. He gave my hand a reassuring squeeze as my father approached.

"Take care of my daughter and thank you for all that you have done for her."

I knew it was difficult for him to say those words, but I really appreciated it and I'm sure Vincent did too.

"Myra is more important for me than you can believe." He said. I felt my stomach become warm and fuzzy at those words. I finally held some sort of importance or place in front of my partner.

They shook hands and then looked down at Myra.

"Shall we?"

"We shall."

◻°•◻◻_____◻◻•°◻

Finally Vincent and Myra will be getting some alone time. Pretty sure these were 5 updates in one week.

There's going to be SOME hot spicy stuff and I hope you're all ready for it.

Please don't forget to Vote, Comment and Share.

Z.A.B

chapter 31

I stepped in after him, feeling a sense of relief wash over myself. I knew why, I had no burden of my marriage anymore. I was free to do what I want.

I was suddenly lifted into the air and spun around. I screamed and laughed a little. Once I was put down I turned around to see the culprit.

"Sam!" I grinned and hugged him tightly.

"I missed you so much." I mumbled against his chest.

"I did too. I'm glad your back to lighten the atmosphere. The last week or so had become unbearable with Vincent impersonating the walking dead."

I laughed again and glanced at Vincent to see him scowling at both of us. "Sam?" I heard sweet voice call out from behind him.

His eyes lit up and he grabbed her hand, pulling her beside himself. "Meet my girlfriend, Ria." He introduced. I held my hand out to her.

"I'm Myra. Vincent's...-"

"Girlfriend." He interjected, coming to stand beside me. I blushed profusely and then nodded. She shook my hand timidly and then hid behind Sam. She was looking up at Vincent warily. I elbowed him in the stomach and he grunted.

He rolled his eyes at me. "Hi, Ria." He greeted and she nodded a little. "I'm going back inside." She mumbled.

As soon as she disappeared inside again I gushed excitedly. "She's so cute, Sam."

"Yes. She is. She is a little shy, but holy fuck. It's so hot."

I smacked my hands over my ears, not wanting to hear the details. He laughed again crossing his arms. "I'm going to bed, I'll see you in the morning. Vincent I need to speak to you."

He shot me an apologetic look and I took the message and retreated, going upstairs to his room. I had intense butterflies in my stomach as I entered. It looked the same, but different. I was not his captive anymore, but his girlfriend.

I felt his strong arms wrapping around my stomach pulling me back into his hard chest. "Why are you just standing here?" He asked, his breath tickled my ear. I shivered at the sensation. I pulled out of his arms and stepped in further turning to face him. He stepped in shutting the door and locked it.

My heart fluttered and I gulped. I crossed my arms self-consciously. When he turned to look at me, his eyes were already dark. It felt like the temperature in this room had been turned up. He stepped towards me and I stepped away, a dark smile made its way on his face.

He didn't stop his approach until my legs hit the bed. His fingers pushed down on my shoulder and I fell back on the bed, backing away from him.

When he placed his knee on the bed I rushed away from him getting on my hands and knees.

It was as if he anticipated my plan and quickly grabbed my hips and dragging me back to him. He wrapped his arms around me and positioned me so that I was in the middle of the bed with my head beside the pillows. His bigger body leaned over mine with his crotch pressing against my butt.

"Why are you shaking, baby? Scared?" He teased, slowly grinding his hips to my bottom. I whimpered, arching to get a better feel of him. I shook my head at his question. He sat me up on my knees, pulling my shirt up. I raised them and he pushed my shirt off my body. He didn't waste a second before cupping my boobs, I gasped leaning my head back against his chest.

He turned me around, pushing me back so I was flat against the bed. He watched me with hooded eyes, hooking his fingers into the sides of my leggings. I lifted my hips, not meeting his eyes as he slid them down, throwing them on the floor.

"Fucking hell, Myra." He groaned, sliding his rough hands up my thighs. I hid my stomach from him, I knew I had lost weight but it still didn't look that attractive.

He grabbed my wrists and pinned them to the pillow.

"Don't hide yourself from me. I want you, Myra. Every single part of you, even parts you think are flawed." He confessed. My lips parted with surprise, it was so heartfelt that I noticed that his cheeks were a little pink. "You're... blushing." I gasped. "Shut up." He grumbled. I giggled, cupping his cheek in my hand and pulling him down.

"You're so cute." I smiled, kissing his lips. He pulled away and smirked. "Let me show you how cute I really am."

He ripped his shirt open, causing the buttons to fly all over the place. I bit my lip and smiled. I really was lucky. He unbuckled his pants and slowly pushed them down his hips revealing his black boxers. I wrapped my arms around his neck and pulled him down on top of me pressing my lips against his. I wrapped my legs around his back pressing myself against him, whimpering.

"Fuck." He groaned as ground his hips against mine. I moaned, pushing my head back against the pillow. Everything began to feel hot, his hands didn't leave any part of me untouched. He turned us over so that I was straddling him. He smirked up at me as if challenging me. I closed my eyes and instinctively rubbed myself over his hard on, placing my hands on his chest for stabilty. I angled my hips so that he slid right against my clit. It had been so long since we had touched each other that I felt ready to explode.

He sat up, leaning back on his arms and I opened my eyes to see his eyes trained on our lower halves. "Good girl. Just like that." He praised and I felt myself clenching on nothing, those words made my stomach flutter.

He turned us over again, pulling my underwear down my legs. He pinned me down again spreading my legs.

"You don't even need foreplay, you're so wet."

I froze.

Those words sounded so familiar. I began panicking when his fingers slid through my slit. Instead of pleasure, dread settled in my stomach. I whimpered, pulling my hands out of his grip.

Tears filled my eyes, and he eventually released my hands. I shoved him off hard and scrambled off the bed. A loud groan of pain pulled me out of my panic. I grabbed the blanket and watched him sit up from the bedside.

"Vincent?" I asked, tears dripping down my face.

"What happened?" He asked sitting on the bed.

"I- I don't know. I think... I think he said the same words to me. I'm so sorry I freaked out."

His face turned deadly. "Come here."

I sniffled and hesitantly approached the bed, holding the thin blanket against myself tightly. Once I settled down beside him, he stared at me now more upset than angry. "Perhaps I should've been more mindful. I'm sorry."

"I didn't mean to shove you. It felt like I wasn't here anymore." I explained shakily.

"It's okay. Come, let's sleep. We will work through this."

Could we work through this? I couldn't even remember anything, maybe it would be easier if I asked him what he saw. I turned away from him and laid down. I was upset with myself. I didn't want my past to disturb any part of my future anymore. I just need to remind myself that I am safe. With him.

▢°•▢▢_____▢▢•°▢

Cockblocked by trauma. Poor Myra.

I'm posting the last chapter tomorrow, or the day after depends when I finish. Kinda filler chapter IMO. I tried to make it as hot as possible, but idk I'm not really feeling it.

Let me know what you think

Please don't forget to Vote, Comment and Share.

Z.A.B

chapter 32

"They want to meet you."

"Today?"

"Yes."

I chewed on my lip with worry.

"Oh and um... we have to leave in an hour."

One hour? I glared at him as viciously as possible, but was just amused. My glare faltered, I didn't have time to argue with him.

"I don't even have anything to wear. They are going to hate me. Oh God!" I panicked, striding over to the cupboard.

Vincent came and stood beside me looking through the clothes. He pulled out a black dress and held it out against me.

"This will do." He stated.

I went to change in the bathroom, earning myself a disapproving look from him. I huffed in response, I wasn't going to change in front of him after he suddenly broke the news to me.

I pulled the dress on carefully, sliding it up my body and pushing my arms through the plain puffy laced sleeves. The sleeves were see through, but the rest of the dress had black satin underlining the lace. It was beautiful. I stepped out, not bothering to show him how it looked and went straight to my vanity.

"No." He grumbled.

My heart dropped, he didn't like it on me.

"You look too sexy in this."

I blushed again, but decided to ignore him again. I minimalistic make up, just some eyeliner, lip gloss and obviously a little bit of base.

I knew I didn't take long to get ready, but it wasn't enough time for my mind to prepare. I grabbed the sterling silver earrings and put them on.

Maybe black pumps would look nice with this. I looked in my cupboard again and put them on. Fortunately I was done in thirty minutes and waited for Vincent. He had disappeared halfway when I started my make up.

The bathroom door opened and he stepped out in a completely black suit. I almost drooled. His top buttons were undone, but he still looked so sleek. No, no dirty thoughts. I didn't want to ruin my clothes.

"Ready?" He asked, I quickly averted my gaze from his tailored suit and nodded. I stood up, taking a deep breath and walked ahead of him towards the door.

I squeaked. His arm slid around my waist, pulling me against his chest. His other hand gripped my neck, tilting my head back as he gazed down at me. I gulped nervously and I knew he had felt it.

"You're getting more and more feisty, baby-girl. I won't be so nice about it in future."

His thumb slid over my glossed lips lightly, careful not smudge it. My heart was pounding at this point, I wasn't sure if should feel threatened by his words. He wouldn't really hurt me.

"I'm- I'm-"

"Shhh..." He turned me around, pulling me against himself again. His hands slid to my bum and squeezed my cheeks hard, pressing his erection to my stomach. I gasped with surprise.

"I didn't tell you sooner because I knew you'd worry. I would've told you last night, but there were more important things to worry about. Neither of us woke up until the afternoon, which is the only time I could have told you."

I looked away. It was my fault. If I hadn't reacted like that, everything would've been normal. My lip trembled.

"Myra." He scolded gently. I pulled away but he wouldn't let me go. He leaned down, holding my chin between his thumb and finger and kissed me, not deepening it. It was a simple kiss. I pulled my self up to my tiptoes, even with my heels I couldn't completely reach him and pressed my lips harder, but he pulled away.

"We should leave now. If we don't, then we won't make it at all."

I frowned at his words. What did that mean?

"Why?" I asked innocently.

I watched as his eyes trailed up my body, staying on my chest before meeting my eyes. I shivered at heat in his eyes, it was burning me. I understood why.

"R-right. Let's go." I stuttered, backing away from him. He smirked and took a step towards me. I bolted out of the room.

He didn't make a move to catch me, we both knew it wouldn't take him long to do so. He came down a few moments later walking ahead of me, twirling his car keys around his finger.

I noticed him standing by the passenger door holding it open for me. I was confused.

He sat down on the driver seat. "You can drive?" I asked surprised.

He looked taken aback by my question and glanced at me. "Of course." He rolled his eyes at me.

"Oh."

"I normally have a driver because I hate sitting through traffic. He knows all the short cuts and plans ahead of time."

"That makes sense." I mumbled. He backed out of the garage once the door slid up, turning his body as he kept one hand on the steering wheel and the other behind my seat. Oh God. What was wrong with me? He glanced at me once more and I quickly looked away.

How could I find him driving so hot? I peeked at him again. He was sitting back, relaxed keeping one hand on the steering and the other resting on his thigh. I clenched my thighs together, my panties were going to be soiled by the time we reach his house.

A few minutes into the journey, his hand landed on my knee, stroking it before sliding a little higher. I looked outside, resting my arm on the window. It slid under my dress, squeezing my inner thigh. For a moment I stopped breathing, but his hand didn't stop there. His finger brushed over my underwear before stopping. He probably felt how wet it was.

"Shall we take a break?" He asked. I looked at him confused.

"Why?" I asked hesitantly.

"To take care of your hot, wet pussy."

I expected him to smirk or laugh, but he was completely serious. His crude words struck right to my core, making me squeeze my thighs around his hand. He took that as sign to continue, touching my panties. I grabbed his hand, stopping him from going any further.

"No... not here." I breathed, holding on to the last threads of my willpower. He didn't move his hands and neither did he say another word.

We slowed down as we drove into a private property area with gates. They opened automatically and we followed the path along the driveway, parking on the side. My mouth dropped open as I caught the sight of the mansion. It was huge. You could fit a small village here.

He stepped out and opened my door, holding his hand out for me.

"Your family lives here?" I asked dumbfounded.

"Yes."

He began to lead me up the porch and I stopped. The nerves began to set in. They wouldn't like me. I'm far too simple and own nothing.

"What's wrong, Myra?" He asked confused.

"I don't think... they will like me." I mumbled, pulling my hand out of his.

"They will. Trust me. And if they don't, we will leave straight away. Okay?" He assured me, taking hold of my hand.

I didn't say anything and began focusing on calming myself. My other hand was already shaking. He rang the door bell and almost instantly the door opened.

"Master Vincent, Madam." An elderly butler greeted, bowing down slightly.

"Thank you, Charles."

We both stepped in and the door closed behind us. There was no way out. Two women stood a few feet away from us and Vincent released my hand walking up to them.

They were definitely not related to eachother, one was Caucasian and the other was Middle-eastern. He kissed both of them on their cheeks and stepped away. They both gazed at me in silence and I cowered away under their scrutiny.

I peeked at Vincent who pursed his lips and both of them and shook his head. Both women looked at each other and burst into laughter. I looked down ashamed, they were laughing at me. I had to keep it together.

I gasped when I was suddenly engulfed into a tight hug from both of them. I looked at Vincent with wide eyes who just smiled a little. They both pulled away, a guilty smile playing on their lips.

"Sorry we scared you. It's the first time ever Vincent brought a woman for us to meet. We just had to try it."

I sighed, feeling as if a weight had been lifted off my shoulders and smiled back.

"It's nice to meet you. I'm Myra." I introduced shyly.

"I'm his Step-Mother."

"And I'm his actual Mother. Now come on in."

They both urged me into the lounging area with him followed behind us closely.

"Please meet the newest member of our family; Myra." They introduced.

Vincent grasped my hand in his, squeezing it gently. "Hi." I waved awkwardly.

An older man stood up and walked towards us. "It's nice to meet you. I'm Vincent's Father." He took my other hand and brought it up to his mouth, giving it a kiss.

"I'm Myra Rahim." I said giving my maiden name.

"Rahim, you say?" He questioned, raising his eyebrow. I nodded.

"Interesting."

"I see you have met my lovely wives." He grinned.

"Wives?" I repeated with wide eyes.

"Yes. I couldn't live without either and they are both okay with it."

I toned down my reaction and nodded, trying to hide the shock I felt.

"Oh please meet my daughter in law."

Just then I heard a familiar voice.

"Meerah?" I asked.

"What's all this fuss about?" She asked, until her eyes landed on me and widened.

"Myra?" She said with excitement. I smiled and she ran up to me, pulling me into a hug too.

"What are you doing here?" She asked, grabbing my shoulders. "She's with me." Answered Vincent.

"With you? You're married to Ben, no?" She said loud enough for everyone to hear. I gulped and look down.

"She's married?"

"No. She was married. Now a widow." He clarified and then there was silence.

"Oh well, good riddance." Said Meerah. She pulled me by my hand and sat me down on the sofa. After the awkward introduction, everyone finally settled down. I formally met Zaheer again, who was still the same, brooding and intimidating. Zaheer had a younger sister named Aliya who was also quite loud. Vincent was an only child, but he got on really well with his step-siblings.

"Let me show you around, Myra."

I looked at him gratefully and stood up, not wanting to be the center of attention anymore. He linked our fingers together and walked me out of the room. I took a deep breath of relief.

"You okay?" He asked, pulling me out of my thoughts. I nodded and smiled.

"You didn't tell me anything about your family. I'm just surprised, that's all." I mumbled.

He shrugged in response. "I didn't think it was important."

I sighed, I wasn't annoyed though. They were really nice.

"You've never had a girlfriend?" I asked curiously.

"Not officially."

"Why?"

"They were not you." He answered.

"But you have..." I paused.

"Yes. I have. But not as often as you think. It was occasional." He stated. I nodded, not asking him anymore. He had no reason to lie to me about it, so I believed him.

He stopped outside a door and opened it for me. I looked inside. It was so neatly decorated and the colours looked great. It was all in different shades of grey.

"This was my room."

"It's lovely." I complimented and walked towards the full length mirror. He came up behind me wrapping his arms around me, holding me in silence with his chin resting on my shoulder.

"Is there a reason you moved out?" I asked.

"Too crowded."

I could understand that. They were all very talkative compared to him. I looked at our reflection to see him watching me intently and I began feeling shy all over again.

"You're so beautiful." He mumbled, kissing my shoulder. I smiled at the compliment. It was nice to hear something good about myself.

One arm stayed wrapped around my stomach and the other slowly trailed down the front of my dress, staying the edge. My eyes followed every move, his fingers disappeared under the edge pulling my dress up. I bit my lip, grasping the arm around my stomach.

Slowly he bared my plain underwear to our eyes. I looked at him and his smoldering gaze met mine before looking back down. I closed my eyes and tensed when his fingers slid into the top of my underwear.

"Look in the mirror, Myra." He ordered.

I gasped and opened my eyes looking at his hand. Luckily my underwear covered my lower half, so I wasn't completely embarrassed. His fingers reached my wet clit and slid over it, rubbing it in slow circles. My lips parted and I moaned as pleasure coursed through my body. His pace was keeping me on the edge, he knew what I wanted.

I raised my hips, rotating my hips in time with his fingers, but that was not enough either. I leaned my head back, unable to hold it up any longer. My knees shook as the pleasure built in my stomach.

"Please." I whimpered helplessly.

He quickened his movements and I gasped, panting for air.

"I think I'm going fall." I warned teetering at the edge of my orgasm.

"I've got you, baby. Cum for me." His arm tightened around my stomach. My whole body convulsed harshly and I moaned again, releasing over his fingers. He didn't stop, but slowed down when I clenched my legs together.

"Good girl. Ride it out." He groaned lowly. My knees collapsed under me and he quickly wrapped his other arm around me, holding me up. He walked us backwards to his bed and sat me down on his lap.

I wrapped my arms around his neck and held him, my heart still pounding in my chest.

A sudden knock startled me and I feared that someone might have heard me.

"Dinner is ready."

"We'll be down soon." He answered.

"Are you okay?" He whispered, kissing the top of my head. I nodded in response.

I cooled down after a few minutes and pulled away from his neck.

"I don't think there is anything sexier in this world than your face when you cum." He smirked, his grey eyes twinkling with mischief.

"Stoppp." I whined hiding my face behind my hands. He laughed again and hugged me a little tighter.

"Let's go down. Everyone's probably waiting."

I took another deep breath and nodded. We both went to the bathroom and cleaned ourselves up before heading back to everyone crowded around the dinner table.

☐°•☐☐_____☐☐•°☐

We were on our way back after spending majority of the time there. Everyone was very kind. His family was very different from what I imagined them to be like. I mean his father had two wives, which was obviously illegal but who would even bother telling anyone else.

It made me wonder if I would ever be enough for Vincent. A lot of relationships are reflections of what their parents relationships are like. Would he get bored of me? It scared me. I don't think I could ever move on from him. I can't imagine my future without him in it anymore.

I love him.

I love him too much to let him go.

The thought of us breaking up, or him finding a new partner dampened my mood severely. Maybe I was overthinking. How could anyone guarantee love lasts forever?

We reached home close to midnight and both of us made our way to our room. He went straight to the bathroom and I stood by the window and looked outside. The cold air blew in the room and the stars glimmered in the sky. There was hardly any light pollution here and the sky was clearer than in most areas in England.

"What's wrong, Myra?" He asked gently, taking my hand in his.

I shook my head in response.

"Tell me, baby." He coaxed, cupping my cheek in his hand.

"Will I be enough for you?" I asked quietly, looking into his eyes. His eyebrows furrowed with confusion.

"Why do you ask?" He enquired surprised by my sudden doubt.

"Your Father has two wives... I know they are happy and it's their choice, but do you think you would...- do you see me with you in future?" I stumbled over my words, hoping that he would understand what I was trying to say.

He sighed releasing me completely and took a step back. I bit my lip, knowing what that meant. I looked back outside, hiding that my eyes were filling with tears. I wiped a tear that fell from my eyes, gulping down the lump forming in my throat.

"Myra." He called gently. I turned to look at him, but instead of finding him standing in front of me, I found him on his knee in front of me. My mouth dropped open.

"I only see myself with you in future and if you're not there then I don't want it. You're more than enough for me."

He produced a small velvet box from his pocket and opened it.

"I'm not proposing yet, but it is a promise that one day when we're both ready I will ask you to marry me.

It is a promise that I will do my best to keep you happy.

It is a promise that I will only want you in my life.

And it is a promise that... I will only love you, until my last breath and in the hereafter.

I want everything, only if you will have me?"

Tears just continued to spill down my cheeks and I struggled to answer him. I wiped my tears quickly and nodded. "Yes." I cried.

I fell on my knees in front of him and hugged him tightly. "I- I love you too." I whispered in his ear. I felt his breath hitch and he wrapped his arms around me tightly.

I pulled away unable to keep a grin off my face with excitement and happiness. He grasped my hand in his and I looked down to see him slide the ring onto my Ring finger.

"It's a family heirloom, passed down for generations. I never thought I would ever find anyone to give it to." He stated softly, kissing the back of my hand. He smiled at me with genuine happiness shining in his grey eyes.

"I love you, Vincent." I whispered again.

"I love you too, Myra." He responded, grinning. We both grinned like fools before I threw myself at him again.

I finally had the love that I craved, who knew I would find it with my captor?

˚•☐☐_____☐☐•˚

Omg. I'm actually kind of crying that it is over. I just want to say thank you to all my readers that gave this book a chance and habe stuck by me from the beginning.

I almost gave up writing it because I felt like the plot was going no where, but I finally had something. I love you guys so much for supporting me and being there during my ups and downs.

This is the first ever book I have completed. It started from a short story to a full 32 chapter book. I can't believe it. Literally no amount of gratitude will be enough.

Thanks again guys.

Please stick around for any other books I might write. I'm thinking of starting another one-shot book again, but obviously back it up this time. Let me know what you think.

Lots of love

Z.A.B

Completed on 30th July 2022 at 06:15am (UK Time)

Chapter 33

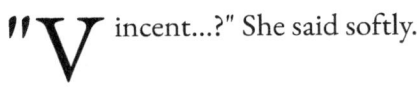

"Vincent...?" She said softly.

"Hmm?"

She sat up beside him, seeming reluctant to ask her question.

"What is it?" He asked stroking her cheek.

"Can I go to see my parents?" She pouted, leaving no choice to agree.

"When will you be back?"

"In a few days. I'll text you." She smiled, placing her head on his chest and closing her eyes. She could tell that he was a little reluctant to let her go, but believed it was only because he was worried about her safety. It hadn't been that long since everything had happened, only less than a month had passed.

Later that day, Vincent sat in his home office, staring at the paper work in front of him with a brooding expression. He couldn't believe Myra left him.

She could've waited until after his birthday to go, but he couldn't really blame her. She didn't know it was his birthday. Perhaps if she knew, she would've waited for the day after. It had been not been long since she had come back to stay with him.

He remembered a few days after they visited his parents she asked him what had happened that night. She wanted to know every single detail. She still couldn't remember a lot, apart from the short flashback she had. He did recommend her to get therapy, but she refused. She felt strong enough to get through it by herself. It was also pointless to her because she couldn't remember anything. Needless to say, he had been more careful whilst touching her to not trigger any more flashbacks. They had only touched each other a couple of times since then and it was not enough to satisfy his needs, but he waited patiently until she was ready for more.

He shook his head before he got too distracted by Myra's body and had a problem that he didn't want to fix by himself. There were about ten minutes left till midnight and he shut the files and stood up.

His door opened and Sam strolled in with a smirk.

"Hello, Birthday Boy." He chuckled, knowing of his sour mood.

"Fuck off."

He turned around, glaring out of the window sourly. All he needed was to hear her sexy voice and that's exactly what he was going to do. He pulled his phone out to call her, but it was snatched out of his hand.

"Grab him!" Ordered Sam. Vincent froze momentarily and watched as five of his men came in. He backed away glaring at Sam. They all jumped him at once and grabbed his arms tightly restraining him. There were two on each side and while he was distracted with the side ones the fifth man tied his legs together.

"What the fuck!" He growled angrily, kicking at the man in front of him, but it was too late. They dragged struggling Vincent out all the way to his bedroom where he found a heavy wooden chair fitted into the floor.

They forced him down on it and strapped him down tightly. He pulled at the ties, but they were pretty strong.

"Happy Birthday." He laughed and walked to the bathroom and knocked three times.

Another man tied a blindfold around his eyes, blinding him completely. The door shut and locked from the outside and it was silent. He panted after all that struggling and released a frustrated grunt.

"My, my. Someone's angry."

It was a woman's voice, one that he hadn't heard before.

"Your friend told me you were mad your girlfriend went out on your special day." Her tone made him feel patronised and even more angrier.

"Fuck you!" He swore. She laughed at his reaction. He heard a very melodious soft chiming around the room and it was coming closer. He felt her soft touch on his cheek, creating warmth wherever she touched.

"I guess I should start by unbuttoning your shirt." She suggested, running her hand down the front of his body.

"You should start by untying me and I'll make you regret ever touching me. Bitch." He spat, but despite his anger, her soft hands were making his stomach tingle. He shook his head at the thoughts going through his mind. Myra. He thought about her. Only she could touch him like that. Only she could make him go crazy with just one look.

He felt her unbuttoning his shirt very slowly before straddling his lap. He jerked his hips away, but she was sitting right on his crotch.

"She sure is lucky." She mused, running her hands up and down his chest. Her wet tongue slid from his chest up to his neck, where she paused and kissed him. God, it felt good.

"Stop. I don't want to cheat on her." He pleaded, his cock was harder than ever. No woman was able to get him hard anymore like Myra did. Her sweet smile, round breasts and juicy ass. And those thighs. He'd never had a thing for anyone's thighs, but hers were so smooth and a little thicker, just enough for him to grab them and...

"She will never find out, baby."

"Fuck."

She slowly began moving her hips in round motions, he could feel her wetness seeping through whatever she was wearing. She continued to leave love bites on his neck, which meant she was definitely going to find out.

"You're so hard for me." She gasped as her movements became faster. Vincent groaned lowly, letting his head fall back and pleasure coursed through him. He could only blame the lack of sexual stimulation in his life for his reaction, otherwise this meant nothing.

The voice in the back of his mind was screaming at this to stop, but he couldn't do anything. He was completely defenseless. As soon as he was out of these ties he was going to murder Sam. How could he allow a random woman into the bedroom that he shared with Myra. He knew he wouldn't be able to hide this from her. She deserved something better than a man that couldn't keep it in his pants.

Her hands went to his pants, unbuckling his pants and pulling the zip down. She paused for moment before stroking his tented boxers.

"Does that feel good?" She asked teasingly. He refused to answer her again. He was going to go through this silently, not giving her the satisfaction of hearing his voice.

She giggled at his refusal and continued to touch him, just enough to drive him insane. His cock tingled at every gentle stroke. He tried to think about anything, but it wasn't working.

There was a knock on his door which caused her to stop as well.

She stood up from his lap all of a sudden and he heard the small bells chiming away from him, unlocking the door and closing it again.

"Vincent." He heard her voice tremble.

☐°•☐☐_____☐☐•°☐

Heyyyyy. You lot didn't think I would leave you high and dry did you?

Can't have a mafia type book without a cheating scandal can we?

Anyways, thanks for all your sweet comments on the last chapter. Please Vote for my story . I have over 300k reads, but less than 10k Votes (i think) and it would mean a lot to me if you could Vote .

Thanks for reading.

Please Vote, Comment and Follow me!!!!

chapter 34

There was a knock on his door which caused her to stop as well.

She stood up from his lap all of a sudden and he heard the small bells chiming away from him, unlocking the door and closing it again.

"Vincent." He heard her voice tremble.

Her voice had him panicking and fighting to get out of the bonds again.

"Myra, its not what it looks like."

She didn't say anything nor did she move.

"Call Sam. Tell him to untie me." He ordered. She walked towards him, pulling his blindfold off. He blinked in the dim light. She came in front of him, sitting down on the bed opposite him.

"Why aren't you...-"

His words got stuck in his throat when he noticed what she was wearing. It was the floral dress that he had brought for her. It just about covered her ass, leaving her smooth legs bare. Her nipples pressed against the soft material and her waist was naked. She leaned back slightly onto her elbow and gazed up at him.

He heard the same bells chiming and noticed the anklet she was wearing. His eyes widened even more.

"It was you the whole time?" He blurted out.

"Happy Birthday." She smiled a little, giving him his answer.

"But..."

She placed her hand on her thigh and slowly slid it up to her skirt. His eyes followed every movement of her hand. She spread her legs just enough for her hand to fit between her legs.

"But what?" She asked innocently.

His dark eyes were burning with lust. He dared her to continue. She spread her legs a little more, trailing her fingers up and down her wet underwear.

"Take it off." He growled, tugging at the ties again.

"You're in no position to make demands." She teased playfully, but rolled the lacy pair down.

She held them up, for a moment wondering where to throw them. She looked at him and smiled deviously again throwing them in his lap. His hands clenched into tight fists and her heart was hammering in her chest with nerves.

After all this time, denying him of the naughty things he had asked of her, here she was in front of him; wearing a dress that hardly covered her body, touching herself so intimately, teasing him in a way she'd never even imagined.

'Am I really going to do this?' She thought, leaning back again. She spread her legs apart giving him the delectable view of her slick center.

She slid her fingers between her legs once more, sliding them into her wet slit. Her finger were instantly soaked and slowly moved back up rubbing her clit. She looked up at him, still feeling a little shy.

He licked his lips at the sight of her touching herself. "Good girl. Go a little faster." He demanded lowly. She shook her head, giving him another smile. She leaned her head back and closed her eyes as tingles spread from her core all over her body.

She stopped, getting another idea. It was a little risky and maybe he won't enjoy it, but she wanted to try it. She climbed towards him to the end of the bed on her hands and knees, allowing him to looked down her dress.

"Fuck, Myra. You're killing me." He groaned.

He watched her come to stand in front of him, sliding her wet finger tips over his soft lips. He looked up into her eyes, sticking his tongue out and licking the wetness off her fingers. Myra couldn't help but shudder at the rough sensation of his tongue against her sensitive fingertips.

She pulled her fingers back and watched as he anticipated her next move. She climbed onto his lap, with her back towards him. She spread her legs over his lap, leaning her head back on his shoulder. He leaned down inhaling her scent, watching her finger disappear between her legs again.

Though this time, she was grinding down on his erection. She lifted her other hand, placing it on his arm, lazily pulling at the straps. His excitement grew, he was finally going to be free.

"Are you mad at me?" She asked.

"No, baby. Why?" He asked, kissing her shoulders. "Because I got you tied up." She shifted again, straddling him.

"Don't worry. It will be your turn soon." He smirked. She gasped and shook her head. She pulled at the straps, untying one arm. Instead of rushing to untie his other arm he wrapped his arm around her.

When he didn't try to untie his other arm, she reached for it pulling the straps. She got off his lap and stood in front of him.

He tugged the straps off his stomach and his legs, standing up and towering over her. Myra felt tiny in front of him, she was the tallest woman in her family, he was a little taller than her father who was 6ft tall.

She gulped, stepping back knowing that perhaps she was in a little of trouble. "Kneel on the bed."

She bit her lip and climbed on, kneeling in the center of the bed. "L-like this?"

All the confidence had drained from earlier, she wasn't experienced in whatever he had in mind for her.

"Spread your legs a little more."

He watched her obey, her shaky hands resting on her thighs. He pulled off his shirt and threw it on the foot of the bed in case he needed to use it later.

He pushed his pants down his hips and let them drop to the floor. Myra glanced up at his almost naked body and blushed again.

"Like what you see?" He smirked, moving closer to the bed. She quickly looked down again, hiding an embarrassed smile.

He kneeled opposite her, placing his finger under her chin and pulling it up. Not wasting another second, he kissed her slowly at first. She parted her glossed lips allowing him to kiss her deeply as he wanted. While she was distracted he grabbed a pillow from behind her, squeezing it between her legs. She made a sound of protest and pulled away, lifting her hips up.

The mischievous smile on his face had her stomach clenching. "What are you doing, Vincent?" She asked confused.

"Ride it."

"What?"

"I said 'ride it'." He demanded and watched as her blush deepened.

"I don't know how..."

She was honestly confused, what could she do with a pillow? He smirked, grabbing her hips and sliding them back and forth. He could feel the stiffness in her movements, until she felt it slide right over her clit. She gasped, looking at him with surprise. He grinned, but she shook her head timidly.

"It's okay." He assured, leaning down and kissing her before she protested more. Her hands wrapped around his neck, pulling him closer. He loosened his grip on her hips and felt her moving them herself. Every time the pillow caressed her clit, she would moan or gasp.

He was so hard from just watching her. He pushed a hand into his boxers, pulling his cock out and stroking it for some relief.

She pulled away to look down and moaned at the sight of him touching himself. She understood now why he was so turned on from watching her do the same.

"You like that, hmm?" He groaned, watching her hips move faster.

She bit her lip, nodding in response. Her eyes drooped closed as she focused on her orgasm unintentionally.

"Stop." He ordered.

She didn't stop.

He held back a grin, tearing the pillow from between her legs and throwing it away. She let out a whine of frustration. He leaned down and kissed her neck, focusing on leaving love bites all over her sweet body. His hands wandered up her back, unclasping the dress.

She stayed still as he pulled the dress down her arms and torso. "You okay?" He asked, noticing her tensing. "Yes... just nervous."

He moved his kisses lower over the curve of her breast, nipping at her hardened nipple causing her gasp at the slight sting. He was getting impatient to take the dress off her body and tugged the skirt down. A loud tear was heard around the room and Myra froze.

"I'm sorry-"

He ripped the remaining seam of the skirt.

"I've been dreaming of doing this."

"But it was so expensive!"

"But worthless in compared to you." He whispered against her lips. Her breath hitched at his words.

Vincent held the remains and threw them on the floor. He pushed at her shoulder, urging her to lay down. As gracefully as possible she moved her legs from under her and laid back. He pushed his boxers down his strong thighs kicking them off. He leaned to the bedside drawer, pulling out a condom.

Myra squeezed her legs together, intimidated by his size. Would he even fit? She trailed her eyes up from his strong thighs to his toned stomach and wide chest. He was so big and strong.

Vincent watched her face noticing the slight fear, but also the lust in her eyes as took in every part of him.

He tapped her legs gently when he finished putting the condom on. She bent her knees, spreading them a little. He pushed himself between her legs, making her spread them wide enough to accommodate him.

"Myra." He said softly.

She turned her worried eyes to him, gulping nervously.

"We can stop, if it's too much for you."

She shook her head.

"I'm just nervous. You're so..."

He narrowed his eyes with concern.

"I'm so what?"

"You're so... big." She mumbled.

He pecked her lips, sliding his length between her slit.

"I'll be as gentle as possible. Just tell me if you're sure you want this now." He reassured

"I'm sure." She answered, giving him a small smile.

He continued to rub his hard cock up and down, she spread her legs wider, squirming with pleasure. He could feel the heat from her centre. Her arousal was smudged on her inner thighs and leaking over the bed.

Myra closed her eyes, slowly relaxing of him laying on top of her. His hard chest rubbing against her firm nipples causing more tingles to race to her core. His mouth continued to press warm kisses on her neck. Vincent reached between their bodies, aligning himself against her, keeping his fingers on her clit.

He slowly pushed in causing her to tense. "No baby, breathe." He murmured softly. She opened her eyes, inhaling and then exhaling.

"Good girl." He praised. She did it a few more times, he waited and at her next exhale he pushed in with a little more pressure. She gasped as she felt him slip in. It hurt, he was stretching her out more than before. He rubbed her clit gently, circling his fingers over. Her soft flesh quivered around him, causing him to groan.

He wasn't even halfway in and it felt so good. He continued to to rub her and pushed in steadily, this time not stopping until he was all the way in. She took shaky breaths, digging her fingers into the bedsheets.

He was so deep inside her, reaching places that his fingers hadn't. "Vincent..." she panted, opening her teary eyes.

"Shhh. The worst part is over." He whispered soothingly, peppering kisses all over her face.

He waited a little more, before grinding his hips in circular motions. He grunted when she clenched. It started with soft mewls of pleasure and pain. Bit by bit he pulled back, before sliding back in. She moaned louder. The slow strokes caused heat to spread from her core, all over her body.

"Better?" He panted.

She nodded, whimpering against mouth. "Fuck, baby. You're so hot and wet." He groaned, holding her hip. He removed his fingers from her clit holding himself up.

She lifted her head a little, looking down between their bodies and watched as he disappeared between her legs, thrusting up into her slowly. Just seeing it happen had her tightening again, she closed her eyes releasing another moan.

He couldn't hold back much longer, he sped up a little more. Myra dug her feet into the mattress, her hips moving against his instinctively. She held onto his strong biceps before wrapping her arms over his back, digging her nails in. She was a sight to behold. Her breasts bounced with every thrust and their hips met with a soft slapping ringing around the room. The pleasure was much more intense than she had anticipated. Their moans echoed around the room as they worked their way to the climax.

"Vincent!" She cried out.

"Cum for me, Myra. Fuck!" He growled possessively. She held her breath, throwing her head back into the pillow as her whole body tensed and she screamed softly. Vincent felt his own orgasm set off by the sight of her sexy face. His balls tingled and he shot his release into the condom as she continued to pulse around him.

They both panted, holding onto each other tightly.

"Wow..." she whispered after a moment of silence.

"I agree." He smirked. He slowly pulled out of her, feeling her hiss at the sensation. He laid down beside her, their legs still tangled together.

"Are you alright?" He asked gently, cupping her face.

Myra looked up at him, shy all over again. "I love you." She mumbled wrapping her arm around his torso.

He chuckled softly. "I love you too."

Vincent let her rest for a few minutes before sitting up.

"Where are you going?" She asked, feeling her heart drop. Did he have to go to work? Was it important? She didn't want him to go anywhere yet.

"I'm not, you are. Go and pee." He ordered softly.

"I don't need to." She answered confused.

"Doesn't matter."

Vincent got off the bed and waited for her to move. She pouted at him, lifting her arms childishly. He shook his head in mock disapproval and lifted her up effortlessly, with one arm under her knees and other under her torso.

She thought he would leave, but he just stood there with a raised eyebrow and amusement shining in his grey eyes.

She wrapped her arms around herself self-consciously.

"Get out." She mumbled.

"You made me come here, but since I'm a nice person. I'll turn around and cover my ears."

"Promise?" She asked nervously.

"Promise." He grinned. He turned around and stuck his fingers into his ears. Myra quickly did her business and wipes herself clean, washing her hands quickly. Vincent washed his hands too and they both went back to bed, cuddling for the first time with no barriers in between.

"Was it everything you hoped for?" She asked, biting her lip nervously.

"It was better than anything I felt before. Besides, I should be asking you that question. Did it meet your expectations?" He questioned curiously.

She nodded with a smile. "It was much better."

"Next time if you intend to surprise me like that, please tell me. I almost had a heart attack thinking it was someone else." He suggested, rolling his eyes at her.

"I'm sorry." She giggled, kissing his chest.

Both of them closed their eyes, sighing with satisfaction. Everything felt better when they were

www.ingramcontent.com/pod-product-compliance
Lightning Source LLC
Chambersburg PA
CBHW072153070526
44585CB00015B/1116